The American History Series
Series Editors
John Hope Franklin, *Duke University*
Abraham S. Eisenstadt, *Brooklyn College*

Arthur S. Link
Princeton University
General Editor for History

Melvyn Dubofsky
STATE UNIVERSITY OF NEW YORK AT BINGHAMTON

Industrialism and the American Worker, 1865–1920

SECOND EDITION

Harlan Davidson, Inc.
Arlington Heights, Illinois 60004

Library of Congress Cataloging in Publication Data

Dubofsky, Melvyn, 1934–
    Industrialism and the American worker, 1865-1920.

    Bibliography: p.
    Includes index.
    1. Labor and laboring classes—United States—History.
2. Trade-unions—United States—History. I. Title.
HD8072.D846   1985   331′.0973   84-27407
ISBN 0-88295-831-3

Manufactured in the United States of America
90 89 88 87 86 EB   3 4 5 6 7

*For those who still believe
that "in the struggle itself lies
the happiness of the fighter."
(A.S. Embree, 1917)*

EDITORS' FOREWORD

Every generation writes its own history, for the reason that it sees the past in the foreshortened perspective of its own experience. This has certainly been true of the writing of American history. The practical aim of our historiography is to offer us a more certain sense of where we are going by helping us understand the road we took in getting where we are. If the substance and nature of our historical writing is changing, it is precisely because our own generation is redefining its direction, much as the generations that preceded us redefined theirs. We are seeking a newer direction, because we are facing new problems, changing our values and premises, and shaping new institutions to meet new needs. Thus, the vitality of the present inspires the vitality of our writing about our past. Today's scholars are hard at work reconsidering every major field of our history: its politics, diplomacy, economy, society, mores, values, sexuality, and status, ethnic, and race relations. No less significantly, our scholars are using newer modes of investigation to probe the ever-expanding domain of the American past.

Our aim, in this American History Series, is to offer the reader a survey of what scholars are saying about the central themes and issues of American history. To present these themes and issues, we have invited scholars who have made notable contributions to the respective fields in which they are writing. Each volume offers the reader a sufficient factual and narrative account for perceiving the larger dimensions of its particular subject. Addressing their respective themes, our authors have undertaken, moreover, to present the conclusions derived by the principal writers on these themes. Beyond that, the authors present their own conclusions about those aspects of their respective subjects that have been matters of difference and controversy. In effect, they have written not only about where the subject stands in today's historiography but also about where they stand on their subject. Each volume closes with an extensive critical essay on the writings of the major authorities on its particular theme.

The books in this series are designed for use in both basic and advanced courses in American history. Such a series has a particular utility in times such as these, when the traditional format of our American history courses is being altered to accommodate a greater diversity of texts and reading materials. The series offers a number of distinct advantages. It extends and deepens the dimensions of course work in American history. In proceeding beyond the confines of the traditional textbook, it makes clear that the study of our past is, more than the student might otherwise infer, at once complex, sophisticated, and profound. It presents American history as a subject of continuing vitality and fresh investigation. The work of experts in their respective fields, it opens up to the student the rich findings of historical inquiry. It invites the student to join, in major fields of research, the many groups of scholars who are pondering anew the central themes and problems of our past. It challenges the student to participate actively in exploring American history and to collaborate in the creative and rigorous adventure of seeking out its wider reaches.

John Hope Franklin

Abraham S. Eisenstadt

PREFACE TO THE SECOND EDITION

In the more than ten years that have passed since the beginning of the 1970s when I first wrote this long essay, the field of labor history has been transformed. Once mostly the province of labor economists and labor movement activists, labor history has now become a vital component of academic United States history. Labor historians publish their own major scholarly journal as well as several more specialized ones; books written about American working people appear with increasing regularity and several have won prestigious prizes; and many college history departments offer at least one course in labor history. Thus, what was an emerging academic subfield at the time I initially began this essay has since developed into a core component of American history.

As the field has evolved and matured, many of the issues which I addressed in the original version of the essay have been more fully explored. Much that was partly supposition or intuition on my own part a decade ago has been largely substantiated by the research and writing of a younger generation of labor historians. Simultaneously, however, the new scholarship in labor history has also complicated the field, creating new dilemmas as it resolved old ones. To the complexities of ethnicity and race in American labor history which I discussed in the original version have been added questions of gender and culture. Today we ask more insistently than ever, how the relationships between men and women determine or shape the texture of working-class life. Or, how material realities and cultural traditions interact to form human consciousness. What, in fact, is the relationship between culture and class?

Before the emergence of the so-called "new labor history" we had a synthesis of sorts to explain the history of American workers. Those two great labor economists and fathers of the discipline, John R. Commons and Selig Perlman, presented a version of American labor history which made a good deal of sense. Commons described and explained how changes in the extent and character of the market for goods altered the structure of production, the nature of work, and the behavior of workers. Perlman explained how the same historical tendencies led ineluctably to the emergence and triumph of that characteristically American working-class institution, the "pure and simple" trade union. He analyzed how history and contemporary material factors combined to make the American worker predominantly job conscious and to make his union an agency to ration, allocate, and guarantee scarce jobs. In the synthesis elaborated by Commons and Perlman, the mature craft union, as it emerged and developed in the late nineteenth and early twentieth centuries, appeared not as simply one more stage in the history of American labor but almost as the ultimate historical achievement of American workers. Overall in the writings of Commons and Perlman the characteristic worker acted as "economic man" (women scarcely figured in their analyses) whose behavior was unmediated by nonpriced transactions.

The "new labor history" shattered the prevailing synthesis. It portrayed workers who were citizens as well as unionists, women as well as men, Catholics, Jews, and freethinkers as well as wage earners, romantic radicals as well as pure and simple unionists. In the writings of historians as contrasted to labor economists, "economic man" became "historical man," an actor whose behavior was affected as much by ethics as price, culture as environment, tradition as market. But what the "new labor history" ripped asunder remains shattered. Labor history today resembles Humpty Dumpty after his fall, and all academic history's horses and men have yet to put it back together again. Furthermore, we still remain uncertain about how best to integrate the enormous research in labor history of the past twenty years into the general field of United States history. We are thus simultaneously bereft of an acceptable labor history synthesis and a sure strategy for incorporating the subject better into broad surveys of the American past.

What, then, does this revised essay offer beginning or advanced students of American history? Simply put, it aims to acquaint students with the place and role of working people in the American past, to introduce them to a part of their heritage too long and too often neglected. It uses the prolific labor history scholarship of the past two decades to revise several false leads followed in the original essay, to correct mistaken assumptions, and to rectify the neglect of several vital aspects of working people's past. Finally, it asks its readers to address the following questions about labor history raised by the European scholar Georges Haupt: "For whom is this history intended? What is its goal? Whom and what does it serve in relationship to the working-class movement?" As we move closer to answering those questions, perhaps we will build a new synthesis for United States labor history, one which also broadens and deepens our understanding of the entire national experience. This essay has been rewritten as one contribution to that goal.

Melvyn Dubofsky

Binghamton, N.Y.

CONTENTS

The People learn, unlearn, learn, a builder, a wrecker,
a builder again . . . Precisely who and what is the people?

CARL SANDBURG,
The People, Yes

ONE

Workers, Industry, and Society, 1865–1920

Most students of American history have read somewhere of the
potentates—Andrew Carnegie, John D. Rockefeller, Gustavus
Swift, E. H. Harriman, J. P. Morgan, among others—who
owned and administered the economy that by the end of the
nineteenth century had become the most productive in the
industrial world. They have heard of Grover Cleveland, William
McKinley, more likely Theodore Roosevelt and Woodrow

Wilson, if not of the host of lesser politicos who regularly appear and disappear from the pages of traditional textbooks. Other students may have read the work of Henry Adams, Henry James, his brother William, William Dean Howells, Theodore Dreiser, John Dewey, and other literary and intellectual giants of the late nineteenth and early twentieth centuries. But what of Carl Sandburg's "people," the men and women who labored to bind the nation together with steel rails; who dug precious ores and minerals from the earth's bowels; who sweated in front of roaring open-hearth furnaces to produce the steel that shaped America's skyscrapers; who tended jennys, looms, and sewing machines to provide cloth and wool for a rapidly growing population; who toiled among black gangs in the fireholds of merchant ships in order to carry American goods around the globe? Of these people—the American masses—until the decade of the 1970s, less was known and less had been written.

The following pages attempt to introduce readers to the wealth of information we have now accumulated about common people in the American past and to enable students to understand the everyday lives and concerns of ordinary folk. They also suggest questions and problems that still must be explored before teachers and students can truly say that the life of the "people" is no longer a mystery and that workers have a history worth studying.

In any society definition of the term "people" is perplexing. It is a truism that no two individuals are precisely alike. Indeed, individuals are distinguished from each other by physical, occupational, cultural, social, religious, and psychological traits. Still, in most societies it is possible to categorize individuals by class, to distinguish the laboring people from the leisure class, the working class from the middle class, the commons from the aristocracy—in short to separate the masses from the classes. In the United States, however, such definitions and categories themselves present almost insuperable difficulties. For what is most striking about the composition of the American working class in the past has been its diversity and its geographical mobility. Unwilling or unable to remain in one community for any length of time and thus establish roots, divided by differences of nationality, race, and religion, the mass of Americans do not lend themselves readily to definition as a people or a class. On the contrary, the ethnic diversity and mobility of American workers has caused them more to resemble atoms in a state of permanent flux than a class in process of formation.

The structural changes that transformed United States society in the half century from 1865 to 1920, moreover, continuously reshaped the composition of the working class. From a nation that at the close of the Civil War was still agrarian and in which half or more of all adults were self-employed, the United States had become by 1920 an urban nation in which the vast majority of individuals worked for employers. Although the number of farmers and farm workers increased from 1865 to 1920, growth in the countryside failed to keep pace with urban progress. Almost 11 million Americans deserted farms for cities between 1870 and 1920, and of the more than 20 million immigrants who came to the United States, the vast majority also became urban workers. From 1900 to 1920 when the total labor force grew by nearly 50 percent, the number of self-employed individuals, including farmers, rose only 10 percent. By 1920 barely more than 20 percent of Americans were self-employed and only 11.7 percent of the labor force worked on farms. The number of workers employed in manufacturing, however, climbed from 2.5 million in 1870 to 11.2 million in 1920, or close to 40 percent of the work force. Both in its growth and its distribution, then, the American labor force from 1865 to 1920 became concentrated in the primary (extractive) and secondary (manufacturing) sectors of the economy.

The creation of an industrial society characterized by a dominant blue-collar group laboring for wages affected all aspects of life. The differentiation between male and female forms of labor grew sharper, as did the distinction between home and work. Men especially were concentrated in the primary and secondary sectors of the economy, with fully 45 percent of all males employed by 1920 in mining, construction, transportation, or manufacturing. Women, however, were by then largely restricted to the lowest-paid jobs in the clerical, sales, and service fields. Almost one-quarter of women workers were employed in the clerical and sales-service sectors compared to 9.8 percent of all men in the former and 3.7 percent in the latter. By 1920, the era of the typical shoemaker, tailor, or blacksmith who fashioned his products at home or in a shed just outside, had long since passed. The typical male worker in 1920 left home early in the morning and spent the next eight to ten hours laboring in a mill or factory among scores, or in some cases thousands, of fellow workers.

Yet it is also important to remember that the blue-collar labor force was itself diversified. As late as 1920, for example, twice as many workers labored in mines and on construction as in iron and steel mills; textile workers, throughout our period, outnumbered iron and steel operatives, and indeed formed the single largest group among workers in manufacturing. Even more surprising, perhaps, domestic servants outnumbered all other categories of employees, rising above the two million mark in 1910. Females were concentrated in domestic service, and more of them found employment as domestics in 1910 than in industry. Not until 1920 would more women work for wages in the factory than in the home, and even then females had to settle for jobs in a more backward sector of the economy—cotton textiles and the clothing trades.

Between 1865 and 1920 the skills required of American workers also changed. Managerial innovations erased old skills either as new machines displaced highly skilled mechanics, such as occurred with unusual rapidity in the iron and steel industry, or as new techniques of organization separated specific tasks hitherto the responsibility of one artisan among teams of workers, as happened in the clothing trades. But the strong back, paradoxically, was in the process of becoming less desirable than a quick mind or agile hands. The proportion of workers described as unskilled tended to decline, falling to 31.5 percent of the male labor force and 28.9 percent of the total labor force by 1920. Simultaneously the number of workers classified as semiskilled rose appreciably, and such machine operators as the laborer on Henry Ford's innovative auto assembly line, the New York City immigrant garment worker, and the southern textile spinner or weaver formed the largest proportion of the manual, or blue-collar, labor force.

While technological changes eliminated or diluted many traditional skills, they never totally abolished the place and influence of the highly skilled worker. Indeed the most recent research indicates that during the years 1880–1920 the proportion of the labor force which can be defined as skilled, irreplaceable, and autonomous (what some have called the "labor aristocracy") held constant at about 14 to 18 percent. Although specific skills changed and craftspeople came to work in more structured settings under tighter forms of discipline, they nonetheless maintained more independence and authority on the shop floor than their less skilled brothers and sisters. Time and again they also proved to be the cutting edge of working-class social movements, a labor vanguard as well as a "labor aristocracy."

This essay examines how industrialization affected the lives of men and women who worked for wages (our concern will be primarily with those who labored in the primary and secondary sectors of the economy and who formed by 1920 the bulk of the wage-working class) and how they reacted to transformations in the nature of work and the character of life. We will consider to what degree American workers came to share a common set of experiences that defined them as a social class and also to what extent differences of ethnicity, religion, and skill served to diversify and complicate the history and experiences of the American working class.

THE IMPACT OF INDUSTRIALISM

How does one evaluate the impact of industrialism on a worker's life? It is a historical experience, impossible to measure precisely because a worker's estimation of the quality of existence is based to a large extent on his or her past cultural traditions and future expectations. The writings of French and English social historians, however, help us to understand the vast gulf in cultural habits, human values, and forms of work discipline which separates the workers of a preindustrial society from the proletariat of an industrial society. "... The acclimatization of new workers to factory discipline," writes British historian Sidney Pollard, "is a task different in kind, at once more subtle and more violent, from that of maintaining discipline among a proletarian population of long standing." In preindustrial societies life and work seem to flow together, as they grow out of the necessities of nature and the traditional norms of the cultural order. Industrialization, however, divorces work from life, as the imperatives of technology and its machines overwhelm nature and culture. "Mature industrial societies of all varieties are marked," comments E. P. Thompson, "by time-thrift and by a clear demarkation between 'work' and 'life.' ... Without time-discipline we could not have the insistent energies of industrial man ... there is no such thing as economic growth which is not, at the same time, growth or change of a culture...."

A cautionary word is necessary. The so-called transition from a preindustrial to an industrial way of life never occurred at precisely one moment in the past or all at once. It was more a process than an event. It was also a process repeated in individual life cycles as well as in impersonal long-term historical trends, as children in each generation learned to move from the less structured, more habitual, more affective milieu of home and family to the rationally regulated, clock-disciplined, and impersonally ordered universe of the factory and shop. Without doubt, the worker in early twentieth-century America labored and lived in a world vastly different from that of his or her ancestors in Colonial America or preindustrial Europe. For the twentieth-century worker clear lines demarcated work from home, labor from leisure, the bosses' time from one's own.

How, then did the culture of American workers change in response to the demands of an industrial order? Until the 1970s this question would have been hard to answer. Most historians of labor concerned themselves with economic and institutional questions: changes in the supply, cost, and structure of labor; the growth and evolution of trade unions and labor federations; labor law; and notable industrial conflicts. Few, if any, social historians wrote about working people, either because they were uninterested in the subject or sources appeared inaccessible. Thus, it seemed that workers lacked a distinct culture of their own. Then in the mid-1960s a group of younger historians began to study and write about those they characterized as the "inarticulate." As they did so, they confronted formidable barriers. For one thing, they immediately discovered that workers in the United States formed many different cultures. American-born workers brought one set of traditions to industrial society; each particular immigrant group from Europe carried to the new world its own mores and values; and Mexican-, Chinese-, Japanese-, and Filipino-American, as well as black workers each came to the factory from a different background, all of which produced divergent social perspectives.

To comprehend how the culture of American workers was transformed by industry, we must know something of the inner structure of life and work in the preindustrial era. We now know a good deal about the attitudes of American-born workers toward religion, marriage and the family, child-rearing, recreation, and neighborhood and its many associations. We have discovered as much and perhaps more about the cultural traditions of immigrant and nonwhite workers. In fact few fields of United States history have produced as fruitful a literature as the study of Afro-American slavery and the post-emancipation history of black people. At the same time, scores of books and articles about the millions of European immigrants, almost all of whom became wage workers in the new world, described the old world customs the immigrants carried with them, how these traditions shaped their responses to industrialism, and how they recreated stable yet dynamic ethnic communities in an alien environment.

No historian has done more than Herbert Gutman to explore the impact of industrialization on immigrant and American-born workers. Seeking to build a new synthesis from scattered references and hints here and there, Gutman posits a continuing clash in American history between preindustrial and industrial values, as new waves of "traditional" peoples were recurrently introduced to industrial society. He recalls a time when cigarmakers would come "down to the shop in the morning; roll a few smokers and then go to a beer saloon and play pinochle or some other game ... working probably, only two or three hours a day"; of an era when coopers stopped work on Saturday at noon to drink in the shop, while reserving Monday for sharpening tools. Such attitudes toward work caused one manufacturer's journal to offer its readers the following satirical advice: "Run your factories to please the crowd .... Don't expect work to begin before 9 a.m. or to continue after 3 p.m. Every employe should be served hot coffee and a bouquet at 7 a.m. and allowed two hours to take a perfumed bath.... During the summer, ice cream and fruit should be served at 12 p.m. to the accompaniment of witching music." All this was, of course, a far cry from the work discipline of a mature industrial society, in which time was money (profits), and causes one to wonder how easily workers adjusted to such changes in life style.

The strain of violence in American industrial history and the manner in which the American ruling class perceived newer immigrants as particularly prone to violence hint at working-class rebellion against new forms of work discipline. England's experience offers supporting evidence. There, as Sidney Pollard discovered, employers "... used not only industrial means but a whole battery of extra-mural powers, including their control over the courts, their powers as landlords, and their own ideology to impose the control they required." As we shall see in the pages that follow something of the same process occurred in the United States. American employers resorted to a variety of expedients as they attempted to inculcate proper work habits among their employees, especially among the immigrant component. English lessons were offered not only to familiarize workers with the language of their adopted land, but also to instill respect for punctuality and obedience to rules. That many immigrants refused to adjust to the discipline of industry is indicated by the relatively high rate of reemigration among east and south Europeans, especially in periods of economic recession when as many as forty-four would leave the country for every one hundred who arrived.

The English historian Asa Briggs has pointedly observed that "in order to understand how people respond to industrial change, it is necessary to examine what kind of people they were at the beginning of the process, to take account of continuities as well as new ways of thinking and feeling." Here, again, considerable work remains to be done in American working-class history. To be sure, we cannot say with any amount of certainty how workers evaluated the quality of their lives in industrial America until we know more about the values and standards they used in judging society.

ETHNICITY, RACE, AND GENDER

In seeking to understand how industrialization affected the life and culture of American workers, we must first consider the relationships among ethnicity, race, gender, and class. The eminent sociologist David Riesman has observed: "No other large industrial society has substituted color and ethnicity for social class as the basis of stratification and hence tension." Although the American melting pot has been cooking since the nation's founding, it has never had heat and pressure sufficient enough to blend diverse human strains into one indistinguishable mass of American humanity.

Despite Riesman's contention that color and ethnicity superseded class as a basis for social stratification in the United States, it must be stressed that immigrants and nonwhites were for the most part industrial laborers and that their history is inseparable from that of American workers as a class. As the United States Commission on Immigration noted in 1911: "With comparatively few exceptions the emigrant of today is essentially a seller of labor seeking a more favorable market." The immigrants came to American shores in four great waves—1843–1857, 1878–1893, 1898–1914, 1919–1921. The largest waves inundated the country between 1878 and 1914; after 1890 masses of east and south European peoples began to enter American society. The arrival of millions of immigrant laborers and their families (some twenty-five million people) significantly altered the character of the industrial working class.

A few statistics illustrate the impact of immigration on American society. At the start of the twentieth century, 75 percent of the people in Minnesota, 71 percent of those in Wisconsin, 65 percent in Rhode Island, 64 percent in Massachusetts, and 62 percent in Utah had at least one foreign-born parent. Industrial cities exhibited an even greater concentration of first- and second-generation Americans. In 1880 Chicago numbered 87 percent of its population as foreign-born or the children of immigrants. For other cities the comparable percentages were: Milwaukee and Detroit, 84 percent; New York and Cleveland, 80 percent; St. Louis and San Francisco, 78 percent. For the impact of sheer numbers, observe New York City, where in 1910 just under two million inhabitants were foreign-born and another two million the children of the foreign-born. In London by contrast at the same time, 94 percent of the population was from England and Wales.

The statistics of industrial employment tell a similar story. Anthracite mining until the 1890s employed mostly English-speaking workers; by 1919, however, over 90 percent of the miners represented the post-1897 wave of south and east European immigration. The great Carnegie steel plants in the Pittsburgh district employed south and east Europeans as 11,694 of their 14,359 common laborers. And in the textile town of Lawrence, Massachusetts, 74,000 of the city's 86,000 inhabitants were, by 1911, first- or second-generation Americans, with southeast Europeans composing fully one-third of the population.

At times the diversity among the work force reached incredible proportions. The copper mining districts in Arizona on the eve of World War I, for example, employed at least twenty-six distinct nationalities, including Navaho Indians. Later in his life an immigrant Chicago cloakmaker recalled his customary lunch hour: "There were two Italians, a girl and myself, two Jewish boys, Bennie and Gordon, two Croatians, Mike and Frank, two Swedish girls, Ella and Lillie, one Slavic boy, one Bohemian girl, one French widow, one Lithuanian man, one Russian fellow and a Polish girl. We used to sing together, each of us a song in his own tongue." John Higham has placed the American experience in a revealing comparative context. As estimated by Higham, Argentina drew 67 percent of its immigrants from Italy and Spain; Canada obtained half its new people from the United Kingdom and a quarter from the United States; Australia recruited almost all its people from Great Britain. But the United States in the period from 1820 to 1945 drew 18 percent of its immigrants from Italy, 13 percent from Austria-Hungary, 16 percent from Germany, 10 percent from Russia and Poland, 6 percent from Scandinavia, and approximately 30 percent from Great Britain. Such a society created a working class as likely to divide as to unite.

The singular ethnic diversity of the American working class tends to overshadow the role of American-born workers and British immigrants. After all, the eleven million rural migrants who moved to the city dominated the labor force in many smaller midwestern industrial cities, and American-born white men and women filled almost all the jobs in the thriving southern textile industry. Perhaps more important, even in the larger industrial centers with their vast immigrant populations, American-born workers played a vital role. In iron and steel cities as well as coal mining communities, native workers and British immigrants (English, Welsh, and Scots) frequently commanded the best jobs or served as foremen and supervisors, as they also tended to do on the nation's railroads. The relationship between American-born and immigrant workers and between native workers and their employers added further complexity to American labor history.

In some regions of the nation, particularly the South and West, racial factors added yet another divisive influence to working-class history. Black workers everywhere, although in this period they were concentrated in the former slave states, occupied an almost separate caste. Over time those who once commanded skilled positions—always a small minority among Afro-Americans—lost out to white workers who increasingly monopolized the skilled trades. Even where they retained skills and jobs, such black workers earned less for their labor than comparable whites and labored more irregularly. The great mass of black workers, moreover, toiled at the most arduous and dangerous, poorest paid, and least secure forms of industrial labor. And they all toiled in a society which over the period from 1877 to 1920 grew racially ever more separate and unequal.

On the West Coast and in the several Rocky Mountain states, Asian immigrants—first Chinese and then Japanese—formed an exploited, low-wage labor force. There, they often met violent resistance by white workers, which culminated in 1882 in the legal exclusion of Chinese immigration. More than sixty years ago the labor economist Selig Perlman wrote that the Chinese Exclusion Act of 1882 "was the most important single factor in the history of American labour, for without it, the entire country might have been overrun by Mongolian labour, and the labour movement might have become a conflict of races instead of classes." Hyperbole, certainly, but it also illustrates the virulence of racism in theory and practice.

And then there were the "ladies." Although the largest single number of women toiled for wages inside the homes of others, ever larger numbers sought and found waged employment outside the household in factories, mills, and shops. Between 1870 and 1920 the number of female factory workers rose from 324,000 to 2,229,000. By the latter date there were more than 8,600,000 women wage workers with almost 50 percent of them clustered in sales, service, and clerical occupations, what later commentators would call a "pink-collar ghetto." Most of these women workers were young, single, widowed, or the wives of disabled or disappeared spouses.

Most male workers believed that married women belonged in the home. They subscribed to the concept of separate spheres—the domestic arena belonged to women, the public realm of work to men. As a consequence of such beliefs, many craft unions denied membership to women and state factory laws closed certain occupations to females. But sometimes even in their separate domestic spheres, married women participated in an underground form of paid labor, either by taking in boarders or homework. Whatever sort of work they did, women, like nonwhite workers, earned much less than white male workers.

The result of all this was a segmented labor force in which members of one sector did not easily move into another. At the top of the labor hierarchy were the craftsmen in the construction and printing trades and the more highly skilled workers in the heavily capitalized, less competitive sectors of industry. Generally English-speaking, north European or American in origin, and Protestant in religion, they were well-paid, relatively secure in their jobs, and enjoyed what came to be called an American standard of living. Beneath them in the more concentrated and less competitive sectors of enterprise were the great mass of semi-skilled workers in the basic and associated industries. Mostly non-English speaking, increasingly south and east European in origin, and Catholic in religion, they earned minimal wages, lacked job security, and lived on the margin of poverty. And beneath them were most nonwhite and women workers, who labored for the most competitive firms, experienced exceedingly irregular employment, and rarely earned a living wage. They were what later generations would call the working poor.

Ethnic diversity and labor force segmentation as causes of working-class disunity were further compounded by the refusal or the inability of American workers to sink durable roots. No scholar has done more to uncover the reality of working-class mobility than Stephan Thernstrom in a study of social mobility among a small group of unskilled day laborers in Newburyport, Massachusetts, from 1850 to 1880, in essays based on other evidence, and, more important, in a book on Boston's working class from 1880 to 1970. For Newburyport, Thernstrom discovered that fully 90 percent of his original sample disappeared from the city at some point in the thirty-year period, the largest number vanishing in the course of the first decade. The experience of Boston workers confirmed the extent of spatial mobility—with one important difference: as a larger city, Boston provided more geographical space for its workers to change residence and yet still reside eventually somewhere inside the larger metropolitan district. Other scholars, through the application of similar statistical techniques, have also found a similar pattern of working-class residential impermanence in several smaller industrial cities.

Although constant geographical movement clearly affected working-class history in industrial America, the precise impact of spatial mobility remains debatable. One might naturally assume that such restlessness among vast numbers of workers could only result, as Thernstrom and his disciples assert, in social chaos and the complete absence of cultural continuity. Yet we know that despite numerous outbreaks of industrial conflict and violence, particularly during the depressions of 1873–1878 and 1893–1897, American society maintained its balance and moved ahead under a conservative political order. Why? Thernstrom's research, perhaps, provides one answer. The majority of the drifters were not the more talented, the more ambitious, the soon-to-be successful; rather they were the failures, the frustrated, the unfortunate, who in the nineteenth- and twentieth-century American social order formed, in Thernstrom's words, "a group of permanent transients, buffeted about from place to place, never quite able to sink roots and to form organizations." Consequently, most American workers never came to know each other in a common setting and thus to develop bonds of solidarity or group antagonism to those above them socially. These wandering laborers, immigrant and American-born, seemed "alienated but invisible and politically impotent, minimiz[ing] the likelihood of effective organized efforts to reshape capitalist society." Meantime, those who actually settled down in a community tended to advance the occupational and material fortunes of themselves and their families, benefiting from the established order and so bolstering it either through action or apathy.

This explanation for the cohesion of the social order in the face of enormous population movement may be valid. Yet it is based to a large extent on a set of unproved assumptions about human behavior. One major assumption is that the possession of property in the form of homes or savings satisfies individuals with their place in the existing social order. Another premise assumes that limited occupational mobility for the parent and somewhat greater opportunity for the children tends to the same effect. Both assumptions seem logical, but remain untested. Indeed, if true, one is left with a remarkable conundrum: a society with, in theory, a slender basis for effective opposition to the established order or for the emergence of radical alternatives but one that in fact experienced in the late nineteenth and early twentieth centuries the recurrence of bitter class conflict, the upheaval of Populism, the rise of socialism, and the forging of an American version of Syndicalism, if not a revolution.

Clearly, the reality of American history from 1865 to 1920, as distinguished from apparently logical assumptions about the dynamics of class formation, is far more complicated than Thernstrom's approach and hypotheses suggest. In some cases, spatial mobility was simply a reflexive response to failure by many workers who became rootless, politically indifferent or impotent, and lacked class consciousness. For many others, however, restlessness or mobility was part of a different social process. For many young workers—late adolescents and young adults—it was part of a common life-cycle pattern, the period during which they separated from the families of their birth and searched for a vocation before settling down to form families of their own. For many skilled workers just having satisfied apprenticeship requirements, mobility was part of the tradition of becoming an all-around journeyman, or highly skilled worker. In the skilled trades, especially construction, which were seasonal or had no fixed location, migration was necessary for employment and income. Hence the "tramping artisan" or perambulatory craftsman was a common feature of late nineteenth- and early twentieth-century working-class life. It was also a primary reason the craft unions adopted such devices as travelling cards and special dues arrangements for mobile members. Those workers who moved by choice or necessity could as easily carry with them the message of class solidarity and radicalism as a sense of impotency and frustration. In fact, some of the most migratory workers—coal and hard-rock miners, loggers, maritime workers, and crop harvesters—proved to be among the most radical, militant, and class-conscious of working people. Wherever they went they carried along the notion that workers everywhere shared a common plight and must act together to make their lives more satisfactory. Whether the exceptional mobility of American workers acted more to dilute or to reinforce their sense of behavior as a class is a problem which deserves further investigation.

WAGES AND STANDARDS

As yet we have said little about how working men and women actually lived in the years between the end of the Civil War and World War I. Here, at first glance, we should be able to stand on firmer ground. Admittedly, if it is difficult to measure or perceive how ethnicity and mobility affected working-class culture, it should be simpler to measure changes in the value and direction of wage rates, annual earnings, the standard of living, the number of hours worked, and job-associated accidents. The material history of America has been one of constantly rising real incomes and of a steady improvement in living standards. If city streets were not paved with gold, as some European immigrants and rural American migrants allegedly imagined, certainly there were paper dollars to be had for the working. The United States was indeed a land of plenty, not a place of grinding poverty and unremitting toil.

Historial hindsight furthermore assures us that between 1865 and 1914 real wages and living standards rose steadily and appreciably. The economists who have painstakingly plotted changes in wage rates, price levels, and annual earnings between 1860 and 1914 provide the statistical evidence that buttresses an optimistic version of the material conditions of the American working class in that period. Clarence Long for one, concludes that both daily wages and annual earnings rose some 50 percent over the three decades between 1860 and 1890, one of the largest percentage increases in U.S. history. Adjusted for changes in the price level (in fact most of the improvement in real income for the period 1873 to 1897 resulted from a long-term fall in the price level) real daily wage rates rose from slightly over $1 (1860) to $1.50 (1890), and real annual earnings increased from just under $300 (1860) to just over $425 (1890). Long estimates that over the same period of time, the number of hours worked fell no more than 7 percent, resulting in an average workday of ten hours in 1890, which offers some idea of the basic hourly wage rate, the standard for determining the earnings of most workers. Summarizing the large picture, Long concedes that the growth in wages and earnings was at best moderate and that a period of rapid economic development within an essentially agrarian setting (the American situation between 1860 and 1890) is not necessarily best for workers. Although the demand for labor rose appreciably, the impact of the simultaneous agricultural revolution released a huge reservoir of manpower, which, added to mass immigration and natural population increase, more than satisfied the rising demand for industrial labor. Hence a substantial proportion of the labor flow was forced, and high wages were not necessary to attract an adequate supply of workers. Moreover, Long also estimates that fully one-fifth of the real increase in wages and earnings resulted *not* from rises in actual wage rates; rather such gains were produced because the relatively high-wage, hard-good industries (such as iron, steel, and metals fabricating) grew more rapidly than the soft-goods, low-wage industries (textiles for example) and consequently employed a larger proportion of the labor force. A more substantial improvement in the material condition of the American worker, Long concludes, had to wait until the end of the initial and most rapid phase of quantitative economic growth.

Is Long's conclusion correct? What have economists and statisticians found to be the trend of real wages and earnings from 1890 to 1920, as the American economy matured? At the end of a so-called prosperity decade, (the 1920s), Paul Douglas published a benchmark study, *Real Wage Rates in the United*

States, 1890-1926 (1930). In that volume, Douglas concluded that, at best, real wages stagnated between 1890 and 1926, a finding clearly at variance with Long's observations. Why should wages stagnate after 1890, a period more prosperous, especially after 1897, than the depression-wracked late nineteenth century? Douglas explained that prosperity did, of course, boost wages but that after the outbreak of World War I prices rose even more rapidly and the worker found himself breathless on an economic treadmill. One nevertheless finds it hard to believe that living standards improved more appreciably in an age of depression than in an era of prosperity. To solve that obvious riddle, a colleague of Long's reexamined wage and price movements for the period from 1890 to 1914.

Albert Rees in 1961 estimated that the real wages of factory workers rose 37 percent during the period, or about 1.3 percent compounded annually, a rate slightly lower than that for the period studied by Long and for subsequent years in American history. Once again the overall impression offered by Rees's research, based largely on a more refined cost-of-living index than the one used earlier by Douglas, is of steady though moderate improvements in wages and living standards. In short, by 1914, real daily wages had risen to slightly in excess of $2 and real annual earnings to between $550 and $600. Rees accounts for this unremarkable improvement in material conditions by asserting that a relative decline in the number of new farms and the continuing high level of immigration pumped excess labor into the market. In addition he asserts that the cost of added and improved capital must be covered before real wages can soar, particularly if capital accumulation and economic growth are to be sustained at a high level.

The general and average wage data, however, cloak an exceedingly important distinction between the earnings of the skilled and less skilled. Recent research indicates that the largesse of American prosperity flowed unequally to the more highly skilled. Among the craft workers of the industrial world, those in the United States were indeed "people of plenty." Not only did they earn more than skilled workers in other countries; the gap between their earnings and those of the less skilled was wider than anywhere else. Taking into account differences in the cost of living, much evidence suggests that less skilled workers in the United States earned little more than their counterparts in Europe. Mass immigration combined with the domestic drift from farm to factory to keep the market for unskilled workers loose. The singularly advantaged position of skilled workers built one more barrier against the emergence of unified American working class.

The research of Long, Rees, and also of Stanley Lebergott leaves the reader with the impression that from 1865 to 1920 working-class life is the story of sustained progress, and that the United States was clearly a society founded on relative high wages, if not unlimited opportunity. Hindsight certainly suggests some reason for optimism about the material progress of American workers. This leads one to wonder how contemporary observers of working-class life and the workers themselves perceived the circumstances of existence between 1865 and 1920.

The statistics, charts, and graphs compiled by Long, Rees, and Lebergott offer one substantial and valid version of American reality. An examination of the testimony of working men and women and the reports and records of various public and private investigating bodies concerning the impact of industrialization presents a different and gloomier picture. A committee of proper Bostonians concerned about an alleged growth in prostitution in their city chose to investigate life among working girls. Appalled by the low wages and long hours it discovered, the committee concluded in its 1884 report that "the fact that the girl works hard all day for three or four dollars a week is sufficient proof that she is not living in prostitution; girls cannot work hard all day and be prostitutes too." And a truck driver testifying before the Senate Committee on Relations between Capital and Labor (1883) told one of the senators: "The poor unfortunate laborer is just like the kernel of wheat between the upper and lower millstone; in any case he is certain to be ground." Working-class children did not escape the millstones of industry, which ground down men, women, and children alike.

That workers had to struggle to exist in the late nineteenth century when industrialization was most unsettling, when depressions occurred repeatedly, and when long-term deflation persisted seems sufficiently understandable. But what of the subsequent Progressive era, a time of prosperity? My own research on workers in New York City and on the IWW suggests that workers endured a similarly arduous existence during the more prosperous Progressive years.

During the Progressive era government and private social workers made numerous estimates of the weekly or annual income necessary to sustain a typical working-class family in New York City. These estimates, all supposing minimal health and decency budgets, ranged from a necessary yearly income of $800 to $876 for a family of four, to $505 for a single man, and $466 for a working woman. (Remember Rees reported that in 1914 average annual earnings at best totaled between $550 and $600.) But a series of federal, state, and private surveys showed that the mass of New York's workers fell beneath the recommended minima. In a sample of 10,000 male wage earners compiled by the United States Commission on Immigration, the average yearly income approximated $413, and nearly half the group earned under $400. Women workers, surveyed by the same commission, earned roughly half as much as the men, two-thirds receiving less than $300 annually. In the case of many immigrant families, moreover, the combined annual earnings (husbands, wives, and children) averaged under the suggested annual sustenance budget of $800, and particularly so for the more recent arrivals. The New York State Factory Investigating Commission (1911–1915) found equally dismaying evidence. After a survey of 109,481 wage earners, it reported that the vast majority earned under $10 a week, and fully 15 to 30 percent of the work force, classified as learners, received only $3 to $6. The Factory Commission discovered that in a whole variety of low-wage industries centered in New York City average wages remained well below proposed living-wage levels. Two investigators of female labor in the city discovered that four out of every five women workers they interviewed required outside financial assistance to meet the minimum standard for health and decency set by the State Commission. One woman worker expressed simply but bluntly the substance of her life: "I didn't live, I simply existed. I couldn't live that you could call living.... It took me months and months to save up money to buy a dress or a pair of shoes.... I had the hardest struggle I ever had in my life."

Similar conditions could be found in the textile town of Lawrence, Massachusetts, which led the nation in its death rate and had a shockingly high infant mortality rate as well. Or in the steel milltowns clustered around Pittsburgh, where a reporter noted of the workers' children: "Their faces...are peculiarily aged in expression, and their eyes gleam with premature knowledge, which is the result of a daily struggle, not for life, but for existence." It scarcely took exaggeration for a union agitator in the rubber center of Akron, Ohio, to headline a leaflet, "A Report from Hell." And it was easy enough to stir discontent among miners on the Mesabi Range in Minnesota, where immigrant workers complained that "if our women go to church the priest they say 'What the matter with Austrian women. They stink in church.'" To which another miner added, "If we eat we can't dress, and if we dress we don't eat." One miner with thirteen years experience observed of the prevailing work situation on the Range, "The contract system just kill the man."

If conditions of work and life were abysmal in metropolitan centers and smaller industrial cities, they could often be far worse in isolated coal-mining villages and more insufferable for thousands of unnoticed, exploited, and almost invisible migratory workers. Coal towns in the hills of West Virginia and Kentucky saw coal barons rule their industrial serfs in feudal style, but without any of the reciprocal obligations built into the medieval order. California's migratory harvesters toiled in the state's "factories in the field," where 2000 men, women, and children might share eight untended outdoor toilets, eat and sleep among the millions of insects bred in the resultant human filth, and labor in hot fields in temperatures above 100 degrees often with drinking water unavailable. And if life was hard for

American-born white workers and European immigrants, it was even harder for nonwhite wage earners who, then as now, occupied the bottom-most rungs of the occupational ladder and also were the last hired and first fired.

For what were at best low wages and a marginal existence, workers labored long hours in unsafe environments. As late as 1920, despite a steady reduction in the work week, skilled workers still labored on average some 50.4 hours a week and the unskilled 53.7 hours. Even a reduction in the hours of work could be a deceptive statistic, for such reductions frequently proceeded hand in glove with an intensification in work discipline and fewer breaks in the workday. Where machines replaced workers in industry, the cost of expensive new capital equipment had to be covered by intensive labor and continuity of production. Thus, as late as 1920, steelworkers labored on average 63.1 hours per week, and some of the basic processes required laborers to twelve hours a day, seven days a week, including one twenty-four-hour continuous shift and one day off every two weeks.

The long hours and intensive labor practices combined to produce in the United States one of the highest industrial accident rates in the Western industrial world. From 1880 to 1900, 35,000 workers were killed annually and another 536,000 were injured. In Allegheny County, Pennsylvania (the Pittsburgh district) in one year alone (1906–1907) 526 workers died on the job, of whom 80 percent were under forty years of age and 60 percent were under thirty. Between 1905 and 1920, no year passed in the coal mines without at least 2000 fatal work-related injuries. A similar sort of human destructiveness existed on the railroads. Among railroad men in the year 1901, one of every 399 was killed; one of every twenty-six was injured; among operating trainmen, one of every 137 was killed, and one of every eleven injured.

Such steady and costly human loss usually escaped public notice; there was no way, however, to ignore the mass deaths that scarred American industrial history. Today few if any Americans are acquainted with the town of Cherry, Illinois, where in 1909 a coal-mine explosion took more than 180 lives. Only two years later in New York City, the infamous Triangle Fire in a modern "fireproof" workshop snuffed out the lives of 146 working women and girls. And in the summer of 1917 in Montana 164 copper miners roasted to death in the North Butte Speculator Mine.

In addition to the long hours of work and the ravages of industrial accidents, job insecurity plagued working men and women. Few workers could count on full-time employment the year around. Depressions and recessions brought cyclical unemployment; style and weather changes caused seasonal unemployment; and new machine techniques replacing old human skills resulted in structural unemployment. Regardless of the precise cause, the unemployed worker was left adrift socially. Public relief was usually nonexistent, and private charity either insufficient or offered only on the most demeaning terms. Seasonal and structural forms of unemployment seldom produced public dismay or demands for basic alterations in society's rudimentary welfare system partly because workers customarily experienced and accepted such joblessness and partly because that form of unemployment seldom affected different sorts of workers and geographical regions simultaneously.

Far worse than the customary recurrent forms of unemployment were the economic depressions that ravaged the nation in 1873–1878, 1883–1885, and 1893–1897. In 1897 the economic skies brightened, and the United States entered an era of long-term business expansion and prosperity. For many workers, however, economic security still remained illusory. In 1908 and 1909 a brief depression caused widespread unemployment, and in 1913–1914 an even more severe depression threatened until the demands of war restored the nation's economic health. The extent of unemployment, even during the Progressive era, proved disquieting. After a series of relatively prosperous years from 1901 to 1907, between 1908 and 1915 unemployment never fell below 4.4 percent of the civilian labor force and, in three of those years, hovered at 8 percent or more. In New York State, for example, the state bureau of labor, which surveyed unemployment in June and December of every year, usually found that over 10 percent of the unionized work force was unemployed at those times (admittedly the figures might not be precisely accurate since they were compiled from trade-union records and reports; nevertheless the tendency illustrated is dismaying). And in 1913, owing to the onset of depression and to a series of strikes, unemployment averaged 40 percent among New York's clothing workers and 25 percent among building tradesmen.

Despite substantial recent increments to our knowledge of late nineteenth-century working-class history, many questions remain unasked. For example: As the economy collapsed recurrently did workers come to accept depressions as unavoidable in the same manner in which they seemed to tolerate seasonal unemployment? Is it possible that initially militant and sometimes violent working-class responses turned to frustration, internally directed anger, and apathy, as depression lingered and unemployment persisted? Surveys by latter-day sociologists who have analyzed the impact of the Great Depression (1929-1939) on western European and American societies suggest the latter likelihood. Quantitative questions also arise. What percentage of workers experienced long-term depression-related unemployment more than once? Did workers experiencing depression for the first time react differently from those who had been through it before? So many questions; so few answers.

For many working people in the late nineteenth and early twentieth centuries, poverty was an inescapable fact of life. In an economy blighted by recurrent business slumps, seasonal patterns of production, and rapid technological changes and in a society without guaranteed forms of social insurance, unemployment and part-time employment spelled material disaster. As their primary and secondary wage earners lost jobs, working-class families slipped in and out of poverty. In a study published in 1904 (*Poverty*), Robert Hunter broke new ground by using statistical and sociological techniques to describe the dynamics of poverty. Rather than holding the poor solely responsible for their afflictions, he probed the way in which the American economy and society inevitably produced poverty. Despite occasional moral barbs hurled at the "undeserving poor" and racialist epithets directed at the "new" immigrants, Hunter succeeded in awakening concerned sectors of the American people to the real nature of poverty and making them aware of the different types of poor people and the specific causes of their indigence.

Hunter's findings, though perhaps not as rigorously arrived at as "objective" social scientists might like, lend weight to a more pessimistic view of working-class history. He suggests that at the turn of the century in both Boston and New York City nearly 20 percent of the population was in distress. In the borough of Manhattan, in 1903 alone, some 60,463 families were evicted from their homes—approximately 14 percent of the total number of families in the borough. Moreover, one of every ten New Yorkers ended his life in Potter's Field, the burial ground for the indigent. The single most common cause of poverty, Hunter discovered, was unemployment. "The annual wages of more than one workman in every four," he observed, "suffered considerable decrease by reason of a period of enforced idleness, extending in some cases over several months." As a result of unemployment, old age, illness, dependent youth, and other forms of dependency, Hunter estimated that in the nation's industrial states over one-fifth of the people, or more than six million, lived in poverty. Only a small minority, however, experienced persistent or permanent poverty. For most of the poor, poverty was a sometimes experience, the economic analogue to the common cold.

NEIGHBORHOOD LIFE AND CULTURE

Our images of working-class life in the late nineteenth and early twentieth centuries, particularly among immigrant industrial workers, conjure up pictures of bleak urban ghettoes and drab mining villages. A typical immigrant neighborhood in the Pittsburgh area was described as follows: "Situated in what is known as the Dump of Schoenville, runs a narrow dirt road. Frequently strewn with tin cans and debris, it is bereft of trees and the glaring sun shines pitilessly down on hundreds of ragged, unkempt and poorly fed children." Jacob Riis in *How the Other*

Half Lives paints an unforgettable, dismal portrait of life in the working-class neighborhoods of Gay Nineties' New York. "One could never rise so early in the morning nor go to bed so late at night," Riis wrote of the city's Jewish ghetto, "that he would not hear the hum of some sewing machine," in an area bearing the appearance of "a big gangway through an endless workroom where vast multitudes are forever laboring. Morning, noon, or night it makes no difference; the scene is always the same." When asked to comment on the beauty of Riis's Manhattan, an English visitor observed: "I have never said that Hell is ugly."

Indeed, ugliness was ubiquitous in the industrial city. Working-class housing was at best noisome, at worst positively dangerous to human health. A middle-class visitor to a city slum wrote: "Look up, look down, turn this way, turn that—here is no prospect but the unkempt and the disorderly, the slovenly and the grim; filth everywhere, trampled on the sidewalks, lying in windows, collected in the eddies of doorsteps." An immigrant, himself living in one such neighborhood, pondered: "This was the boasted American freedom and opportunity—the freedom for respectable citizens to sell cabbages from hideous carts, the opportunity to live in those monstrous, dirty caves that shut out the sunshine."

These immigrant working-class neighborhoods bear a surface resemblance to the black and Puerto Rican ghettoes that replaced them. Nonwhite lower-class neighborhoods call to mind social disorder, frustration, crime, drugs—in short, the image of a human jungle. But the immigrant ghettoes of the past, despite their share of crime, chaos, and disease, seemed to breed more hope than despair, more success than abject failure. Jews, Italians, Slavs, and Finns, historians inform us, maintained a wide variety of customary cultural institutions and a substantial sense of community, factors that abetted social and occupational mobility and that rendered the immigrant ghetto a way station on the road to successful accommodation with American society. Among the old and new immigrant workers family and kinship networks, ethnic societies, saloons, and music halls preserved their traditions and provided a culture that sustained their existence in an industrializing society.

Other surface resemblances exist between the industrial working class of the past and the nonwhite lower class of the present. When American-born elites thought of industrial workers in the late nineteenth century, especially of recent immigrants, they often projected onto workers images of untamed brutishness and potential violence. Lacking the well-developed superego of the good *bourgeois* citizen, the immigrant worker, it was thought, easily succumbed to alcohol, sex, crime, and violence. In short, the middle class perhaps projected its own anxieties about sex, drink, and violence onto the working class at the same time that it sometimes perceived lower-class life as more human, natural, and perhaps, happier. In a sense, then, the first generations of industrial workers served a role for the middle class comparable to that played by Harlem blacks for white "slummers" in the Roaring Twenties and by "hip" Negroes for Norman Mailer and "the beats" in the 1950s.

Was there any substance to these middle-class perceptions of working-class life? To be sure, working-class neighborhoods had their share, or more, of alcoholism, family failure, crime, and violence. What working-class community lacked its corner taverns, its teenage street gangs, its adult criminals specializing in providing services considered illegal by Protestant society, and its wife- and child-beaters? All this existed, and in abundance, but its place in working-class culture remains as yet little understood. We do now know much more about the texture of immigrant working-class life and community. Ethnic neighborhoods were neither hells nor utopias. Families did fall apart, as immigrant fathers met frustration and unemployment and as some of the more Americanized children drifted away from their parents and into juvenile street gangs and adult lives of crime. But more often than not the families held together. When fathers lost jobs, children continued to labor or left school to work. Wives took in boarders or homework to help make ends meet. All members of the family pooled their earnings, frequently to achieve one overriding aim—the purchase of a home of one's own—not as a symbol of success or social mobility but as an element of security and material independence. Immigrant families also scrimped and saved to build and support the churches and synagogues so vital to their cultures as well as the ethnic societies which helped them maintain traditional values. Working together, sustaining each other in time of adversity, and slowly but never completely adapting their traditional cultures to a new-world industrial society, most immigrant families built for themselves a modicum of security and stability, however precariously achieved.

DREAMS AND ILLUSIONS: THE PROMISE OF AMERICAN LIFE

Considering the prevalence of poverty, the recurrence of economic depression, the drabness of working-class neighborhoods, the severe shock suffered by preindustrial peoples adjusting to industrial society, one is entitled to ask why workers continued to come to the United States from Europe and why they continued to move from the country to the city. One is equally entitled to wonder why rebellion appeared so rare an event. In some cases the answer is easy enough. Many immigrants and Americans had no choice. Agricultural change pushed millions off the land in the United States, as well as in Europe, and technological innovation rendered many customary craft skills superfluous. To these people new job discipline, hard work, and low wages in the factory were preferable to customary arrangements without work and without wages in the countryside or the artisan's shop. Wages in industry tended, moreover, to be higher than elsewhere in the economy, and within the industrial sector highest in the newest and most rapidly expanding industries; American wages, especially for the skilled, were considerably higher than those paid in Europe. Factory discipline and hard work thus had its rewards, and for some workers, even in the years between 1865 and 1920, the rewards could be quite substantial. Many a skilled printer, carpenter, machinist, or molder could earn as much and live as well, if not better, than a white-collar clerk or lesser professional.

The explanation for working-class accommodation to industry probably lies somewhere in the relationship between what most workers had experienced in the immediate past contrasted to their present condition and future expectations. Here, once again, the available evidence is at best ambiguous. On the one hand, a Jewish immigrant to America might observe: "Even the slums of the days were beautiful to me compared to the living quarters of Lithuania . . . even though the toilet was in the hall, and the whole floor used it, yet it was a toilet. There was no such thing in Lithuania . . . . Here there was running water. I saw horse cars and trolley cars, and when I saw a cable car on Broadway, I thought America was truly the land of opportunity." But, on the other hand, an immigrant working-class girl lamented: "Where was the time for the free schools, where was the time for the wonderful libraries, for the luxurious museums? Where was the opportunity to rejoice in all the blessings of this free country?" Evidence certainly indicates that most recruits to industrial society bettered their material circumstances, that is, their earnings and standard of living rose. Whether or not economic improvements compensated for the exchange of a customary way of life for a less secure sort of modernity seems dubious. Recent research and writing suggest that Slavic immigrant workers were not enchanted by the material benefits of industrialism. Initially, few among them considered themselves permanent industrial workers and they labored in steel mills and coal mines primarily to earn enough money to purchase land in the old country, where they could reestablish their traditional preindustrial way of life. We must also inquire to what extent immigrant and American-born workers reconciled their illusions about industrial society with its realities.

What, in fact, were the illusions that American farm-boys and European immigrants had about urban-industrial life in the United States? Most immigrants clearly did not expect to pick up gold in the streets or become millionaires overnight. Their expectations were much more limited: steady work, higher wages, some chance for occupational advancement, the acquisition of real property. Were the aspirations of first-generation, American-born industrial workers the same? Or were they possibly motivated by more grandiose dreams, hopes of achieving substantial upward economic mobility, even business imperium? In brief, to what extent did workers believe in the existence of boundless opportunity in a free society in which all individuals, despite the circumstances of their birth, rose and fell solely on the basis of their abilities and performances?

Hard evidence about workers' attitudes toward the American myth of opportunity and success is scant. What we do know is what happened economically and occupationally to those workers who remained long enough in one community to be traced by later historians, and we also have some idea of the social origins of America's business elite. It has been shown that although individuals rarely rose from poverty to wealth, most residentially settled workers succeeded in moving slightly up the occupational ladder or in acquiring homes and savings accounts; their children sometimes discarded blue collars for white ones and rose from the working class to the lower middle class. A number of scholarly essays have also proved, as William Miller observed, that individuals who rose from rags to riches have been more common in history textbooks than in actual history. Almost without exception members of the American business elite from 1870 to 1920 did not originate among the working class. Yet Herbert Gutman has shown that, in the case of Paterson, New Jersey, successful local iron, locomotive, and machinery magnates actually rose from the class of skilled, white Anglo-Saxon Protestant workers. Nevertheless Paterson's successful men, its real-life Algers, represented only an infinitesimal fraction of the total working-class mass in the city, and their existence by itself offers no proof that most workers considered such success a distinct possibility. We must ask, What seemed most normal to workers—the few poor men who succeeded exceptionally or the vast group that inched ahead or struggled to stay even? Moreover, as the industrial city grew and its neighborhoods became more segregated economically and socially, what then happened to working-class images of opportunity and success? Indeed, what was more important in determining a worker's attitudes and values—the immediate circumstances of work, family, and neighborhood life, or knowledge of a few men who had made good? This last question is especially pertinent because most recent scholarship on immigrant workers finds that their lives were mostly bounded and defined by their families and ethnic neighbors.

The three chapters to follow consider more fully how industrialism altered the structure of the working class and affected the worker's place in society. They will examine how workers responded to the impact of industrialism and what happened when workers' conditions did not meet their expectations, when they considered the quality of life unsatisfactory, and when they refused to accept the dominant ideology of individual competition for success in the free marketplace. We will investigate why workers protested or rebelled only spasmodically, and we will observe how the evolution of a mature industrial society created a new sort of working class with its own characteristic movements, organizations, and style of action.

"In a land where there is more than enough for all, all should have at least enough."

ANON. (1877)

TWO

Time of Chaos, 1865–1897

The years from the end of the Civil War to the turn of the new century, encompassing the so-called Gilded Age, were for the American working class a time of turbulence and upheaval. Workers fought some of the most violent industrial conflicts in American history; developed the trade-union structures that came to dominate the subsequent evolution of the labor movement; engaged in a fratricidal struggle in the labor movement from which emerged the American Federation of Labor; generated the first wave of nationally known labor leaders—John Siney, William C. Sylvis, Terence Powderly, John Mitchell, and Samuel Gompers; and participated in a wide variety of political protest movements, from the farmer-labor third parties of the 1870s to the Populist crusade of the 1890s and the birth of Marxian socialism in the United States. By the end of the century, then, the United States had matured as an industrial society, and its labor movement had experienced a painful and often uncertain pattern of growth.

THE SHOCK OF CHANGE

That the years of earliest and most intensive industrialization produce the gravest shock to the established social order has become a commonplace observation. American society proved no exception to this rule as, between 1865 and 1897, a whole range of orthodox values and community structures were shattered by the rapidity and extent of economic and social change. Individualism, equal opportunity, democracy, and liberty assumed new forms and implications in a society increasingly dominated by giant business corporations and urban concentrations of population. Clearly, individualism and democracy had different meanings for John D. Rockefeller and for his refinery hands, or for Andrew Carnegie and the men who sweated before Homestead's open hearths. Where once notions concerning equal competition in the economic marketplace among small businessmen, the relative equality and independence of employers and employees, and the existence of communities in which men and women knew and dealt with each other on a personal, human basis across class lines seemed apt, this became less true after the Civil War. Social evolution in the United States seemed to be following the model suggested by the German sociologist Ferdinand Tönnies, in which a society based on *Gesellschaft* was superseding one built on *Gemeinschaft*; that is, formal rules of social behavior, a variety of procedurally proper legal arrangements, and bureaucratic structures that impersonally and mechanically managed society superseded customary norms, law based on tradition, and face-to-face personal dealings as the primary means of community control. Put another way, in industrial society community tended to succumb to society, the personal relationship to the bureaucratic one, the human to the mechanical.

In the late nineteenth century, technology—particularly the railroad, the steamship, and the telegraph—created a truly national economy. Technological innovations were "shrinking the globe" by greatly increasing the speed and efficiency of transport and communications. But material changes seemed to outdistance people's ability to master innovation. Most individuals still lived in what the historian Robert Wiebe has characterized as "island communities," in which customary arrangements and face-to-face relations were the norm. Working people especially, no matter how mobile, preferred to define their lives in terms of family, neighborhood, and church. As a result, the power of the productive forces of the economy greatly surpassed the ability of human institutions to control them more equitably. Phrased in terms made famous by Karl Marx, "the relations of production" had fallen out of phase with "the forces of production." There thus emerged a social jungle in which the ability of the powerful few to dominate the society and economy to their own advantage frustrated the masses who were less adept at technological and bureaucratic arrangements. The failure of political parties and of traditional social structures and relationships to offer many citizens a sense of security, or power, in America's new industrial society produced a chaotic environment, one which at times seemed to border on anarchy.

Nowhere was the chaos of the times more evident than in the changing relationship between American workers and their employers. As recent scholarship, especially the work of Herbert Gutman, has established, workers did not enter the post–Civil War era of industrial expansion as a powerless proletariat. Indeed for much of the 1870s and 1880s workers possessed power sufficient to countervail their employers. In the iron, steel, and farm machinery industries, skilled workers united in craft unions occupied indispensable positions in the production process. So vital were their skills that in numerous cases these workers, either individually or through their unions, determined the pace of work, the organization of the job, and the rate of pay. David Montgomery gives the following description of the work practices of unionized Ohio iron workers.

The workers... decided collectively, among themselves, what portion of [the] rate should go to each of them... how work should be allocated among them; how many rounds on the rolls should be undertaken each day; what special arrangements should be made for the fiercely hot labors of the hookers during the summer; and how members should be hired and progress through the various ranks of the gang. To put it another way, all the boss did was to buy the equipment and raw materials and sell the finished product.

The power exercised by craftsmen also often redounded to the advantage of the larger numbers of less skilled laborers, who received wage increases when skilled workers struck successfully. It was also customary for semiskilled operatives, whether organized in unions or not, to join the strikes initiated by their more skilled brothers.

American workers had other sources of strength in their ongoing struggle with employers for greater security. Workers in smaller industrial cities and mining towns exercised power locally. Often, their sheer numbers enabled workers to control by their votes such crucial local offices as mayor, sheriff, or county judge. In other instances, industrial cities resembled Wiebe's "island communities" where face-to-face relationships and traditional social arrangements prevailed. There local workers could count on sympathy and even overt assistance from tradesmen and professionals whom they patronized and who frequently perceived the aggressive new industrialists as alien influences in the established community.

Industrialists moreover scarcely felt omnipotent. The same technological and economic forces that vexed workers, also perplexed employers. New machines and production processes that obliterated old crafts also destroyed the competitiveness of less efficient or ruthless businessmen. Oil operators and iron and steel manufacturers who were neither as aggressive nor as skillful as the Rockefellers and Carnegies fell to the competitive wayside by the scores. The economic depressions of the 1870s, 1880s, and 1890s, which caused workers to lose jobs by the millions, brought business failure to thousands of enterprises. Unable to control a highly competitive and insecure marketplace or to manage employees as they chose, industrialists, like their workers, anxiously sought greater economic security.

Industrialists followed two paths to economic security. One road out of the competitive economic jungle led into the corporate merger and concentration movement, which peaked between 1897 and 1904, and which effectively reduced competition in several key industries. Another route led employers to exert unilateral authority over their employees' wages, hours, and working conditions. It impelled industrialists to adopt technological innovations in response to economic fluctuations, not the needs of workers. But both paths to economic security were beset with many barriers. The corporate concentration movement conflicted with traditional American values sanctifying individualism, free competition, and equal opportunity; the effort to discipline workers ran up against their indispensable craft skills and their social and political power in many smaller communities.

INDUSTRIAL CONFLICT

As workers attempted to preserve or expand their power and employers sought additional authority over their employees, a series of bitter battles between labor and capital ensued. Students of history must pause and wonder at the roll call of costly late nineteenth-century industrial conflicts: the Molly Maguires of anthracite coal district notoriety; the railroad strikes and riots of 1877; the Haymarket affair of 1886 and its panic-ridden aftermath; the Homestead and Coeur d'Alene conflicts of 1892, in which armed troops ultimately subdued militant strikers; and the Pullman railroad boycott of 1894, in which the full weight of the federal government was pitted against striking workers. But these were only the most notable and noticed conflicts of the era. Many other equally violent and cruel battles occurred on the local level, some of which are only now being described and analyzed by historians. Again and again in these local conflicts, strikebreakers appeared, violence ensued, and state or federal troops intervened. Fifty-five Slavic miners in northeastern Pennsylvania were shot by sheriffs' deputies during the so-called Latimer "riot" of 1892. And in the agrarian South in 1894, the year of the Pullman conflict, coal miners and operators in the Birmingham-Bessemer district of Alabama engaged in a bitter, no-holds-barred struggle. A similar pattern of labor militancy and violence unfolded in the Rocky Mountain mining communities of Leadville and Cripple Creek, Colorado, as well as in the Coeur d'Alene region of Idaho.

Thousands of less militant and perhaps nonviolent strikes also scarred the industrial history of the period. Between 1881 and 1890, for example, the federal Bureau of Labor Statistics estimated that 9668 strikes and lockouts had occurred. In 1886 alone, 1432 strikes and 140 lockouts involved some 610,024 workers. The spontaneity of these conflicts also deserves comment. Again, according to the Bureau of Labor Statistics, the proportion of strikes in the 1880s *not* initiated by unions was probably as high as 39 percent, and, although statistics are unavailable for the 1870s, the percentage of spontaneous strikes was likely even higher in that decade. By the end of the nineteenth century, then, the strike had become the wage worker's primary line of defense against employers' exactions. Together with the trade union, it served as the characteristic form of response by workers to an industrial society, their adoption of new rules for the game. Over the course of the last three decades of the nineteenth century, strikes typically grew more planned and less spontaneous, more often associated with unions than not, and as often offensive as defensive.

At this point it might be well to examine more closely what the history of the late nineteenth century revealed about the changing relationship between employers and workers, capital and labor. A good place to begin is with the history of the most romanticized and violent of the era's labor battles—that between the anthracite miners of northeastern Pennsylvania and the region's mine owners which produced the legend of the Molly Maguires (a legend so potent that in 1969 Hollywood filmmakers found a place for the Mollies in the cinema world). Most accounts of the conflict in the anthracite region tend to be simplistic, for they describe either noble operators protecting the local community against the depredations of criminal anarchists (the Mollies) or courageous miners denied all peaceful redress of legitimate grievances defending their manhood against exploitative and conspiratorial employers. Recently, however, a subtler and more realistic history of the Molly Maguire phenomenon has emerged.

The anthracite district of Pennsylvania experienced rapid economic and population growth during the Civil War and immediate postwar years, as local transportation penetrated the New York City and Philadelphia markets. Prosperity stimulated increased capital investment and attracted thousands of new miners to the district. The result was unfettered economic competition, a collapse in the already shaky community social structure, and a breakdown in "law and order." In the 1860s and 1870s this region of the Northeast seemed to resemble a mythical lawless Western frontier community, a situation in which neither employers, nor miners, nor middle-class citizens could find security.

Miners were among the first to seek a means to restrain unfettered individualism. Overinvestment in mining properties had glutted coal markets, leading operators to reduce wages and discharge workers. Economic insecurity was compounded by the employers' constant surveillance of their workers. "There is no freedom of action or speech among them," commented an observer among Pennsylvania coal miners. "Men dare not be men." Miners, however, sought to reassert their manhood by uniting in an organization, the Workingmen's Benevolent Association (WBA), through which they hoped to achieve cooperatively the security that had eluded them as individuals. Under the guidance of John Siney, the first in a long line of miners' leaders, the WBA from 1869 to 1873 won a modicum of success in the anthracite fields. If unable to achieve all the miners' objectives, the organization did nevertheless place some limits on the operators' authority.

Throughout this short period of relative union power, brawls, unsolved murders, and crimes of violence plagued the anthracite region. Then, when economic depression hit in 1873, the area's social disorganization worsened, as unemployed miners threw a further burden on community resources.

In this environment, employers were not long in reacting to economic anarchy and social disorder. Franklin B. Gowen, president of the Reading Railroad, seized the opportunity to bring order to the district. On the one hand, he sought to reduce competition among the smaller operators; on the other hand, he attempted to discipline the miners by smashing their union. As controller of the only source of transportation from the southern fields to market, Gowen compelled other mine operators to follow his own policies regarding prices, wages, and union negotiations; as a friend and associate of the railroad men who dominated the northern fields, he arranged common price policies and common antiunion tactics. Finally, he quietly purchased all the coal properties available—which was a definitive means to eliminate "destructive" competition in the industry. But one force stood between Gowen and total domination of the anthracite district: the WBA.

Economic depression and community fears served Gowen's purposes. As already noted, the depression had exacerbated long-standing anxieties about law and order. Newspaper reports and community perceptions, if not measurable statistics, made crime seem rampant. Many people were ready to believe the most fantastic explanations concerning the breakdown in law and order, including the suggestion of heinous conspiracies. A conspiracy explanation of local disorder was rendered believable by the ethnic makeup of the community. The first inhabitants of the region had been the Scots-Irish, followed in turn by English and Welsh coal miners. By 1873, these three English-speaking Protestant groups dominated the local society and economy. American-born Scots-Irishmen tended to own the mines, while Welshmen and Englishmen, mostly the former, served as mine superintendents and public officials. As the industry developed, however, a new and disturbing ethnic group—the Irish—came to the community. Catholic by birth and custom, the immigrant Irish workingmen brought with them an abiding hatred of all things British. This hatred was more than reciprocated by the established, and Protestant, British. Both at work and at home, the Irish workers were exploited by their British superiors, adding a centuries old ethnoreligious dimension to the district's basic social-economic conflict.

It took neither a great imagination nor conspiratorial theories to expect that the Irish would seek to improve their place as workers and as members of the community. If Welsh mine superintendents and town deputies harassed their Irish "inferiors," it was only natural that the Irish would, when the opportunity arose, retaliate. Much of the district's violence was thus ethnic in origin, pitting Irish against Welsh. The Irish had brought with them to the United States a history of secret society agitation and action against their British overlords in Ireland. What had occurred previously in Ireland, it seemed only logical to inhabitants of the anthracite district, would repeat itself in the New World. An American counterpart to the Irish secret society seemed to exist in the Ancient Order of Hibernians (AOH), a fraternal society of Irish immigrants and its alleged inner circle— the Molly Maguires—that executed the AOH's covert, illegal activities. By the mid-1870s Protestant residents of the anthracite district believed that such a secret organization existed and that it posed a clear and present danger to the community's welfare.

How the Molly Maguires became embedded in labor history is the story of Franklin Gowen's antiunion machinations. Committed to breaking the WBA, Gowen realized that defense of law and order made a better public platform than antiunionism. Working closely with the Catholic Bishop of Philadelphia and anthracite district law officials, Gowen infiltrated a secret agent, one James McParland, into the AOH. McParland ingratiated himself with local AOH leaders and soon began to submit reports detailing the conspiratorial plans and illegal acts of an "Inner Circle." He remained active among the Mollies for almost two years, participating in their conspiracies and proving exceptionally effective at protecting his employer's property though somewhat less so in saving lives. McParland's willing participation in crimes of violence leads one to wonder whether he was a loyal secret agent simply doing his duty or an *agent provocateur*. Whatever the truth, much circumstantial evidence and McParland's subsequent career as a Pinkerton and an accused *agent provocateur* raise substantial doubts about his method of operation.

While Gowen's secret agent amassed evidence against the Mollies, a strike erupted in 1875 between the WBA and the operators. This conflict, known to history as the Long Strike, lasted from January through April, brought much suffering to miners and their families, and occasioned a sharp increase in the incidence of local violence. Benefiting from rising community antipathy to disorder, himself linking union and strikers to violence, and gaining strength from internal union divisions, Gowen smashed the strike, winning a victory soon to be made unconditional by McParland's revelations.

Less than a year after the Long Strike, McParland surfaced to become the leading state's witness during a series of trials against Mollies in which Gowen acted as prosecuting attorney. The trials followed a pattern: in each case McParland was the key witness, supported by a series of informers, all of whom were later duly rewarded, and in which each jury returned a verdict of guilty. As a result of the trials and the convictions, twenty Mollies were hanged. As prosecutor, Gowen calculatingly staged the trials in a way which linked the Molly Maguires with unionism, placed the community in his debt by crushing lawlessness, and, finally, by identifying the WBA with the Mollies, effectively killed unionism in the district until the emergence of the United Mine Workers at the end of the century.

Gowen's expenditure on the case of at least $150,000 seemed at the time well worthwhile.

At this point, however, it is essential to remember that the struggle in the anthracite fields was *not* exceptional, though the Molly Maguires may well have been. The pattern of conflict discovered by Herbert Gutman and other historians in a variety of working-class communities during the depression years, 1873–1876, bears a marked resemblance to events in the anthracite region. In Braidwood, Illinois, Paterson, New Jersey, Cambria, Pennsylvania, and elsewhere workers struggled to maintain their security and sense of independence against employers who, like the Pennsylvania coal-mine operators, sought to survive depression and falling profit margins by eliminating competition and disciplining labor.

Most industrialists lacked the Irish immigrant scapegoats that Gowen had found so convenient. But they too learned that opposition to violence and defense of law and order could be turned to their own advantage. In case after case from 1873 to 1876, and in fact over the course of the remainder of the century, when employers encountered a powerful local work force, they engaged in tactics which inevitably caused violence. If unable to recruit scabs locally or to attract strikers back to work, industrialists recruited strike breakers elsewhere and hired their own armed guards to provide the physical security denied them by local peace officers. The stark fact of strangers taking jobs customarily held by local workers engendered bitterness and violence. This bitterness was exacerbated by the ethnic and racial characteristics of many, although certainly not all, strike-breakers, who were east European Catholics or American blacks. Ethnic and racial divisions thus compounded economic and social fault lines, in the process raising violence to a higher level. As violence spread and local authorities proved unwilling or unable to control it, employers acted as ardent defenders of property rights and law and order. Local officials might ignore forms of violence whose origins they understood or sympathized with, but state governors and United States presidents were sworn to uphold state and federal constitutions and to preserve law and order. Consequently, in most cases employers could rely upon governors or presidents to provide marshals or troops to preserve the peace. Of course, it was no coincidence that law and order was ordinarily maintained at the expense of the strikers and their unions. Or that in numerous instances workers saw their local power usurped by external sources of authority, functioning, in effect, in the interest of industrialists.

This pattern of conflict and repression can be seen with crystal clarity in the events of the most violent year in the late nineteenth century—1877. Financially strained railroads in 1877 cut workers' wages sharply and also increased workloads. Such an open attack on railroad labor's security stimulated mass anger and a movement to organize railwaymen in one big union; individual discontent, however, quickly outran the evolution of methodical organization. When in July, the Baltimore and Ohio Railroad announced its third consecutive 10 percent cut in wages, a spontaneous walkout erupted in Martinsburg, West Virginia, and spread from there to most other railroads in the northeast and north central states. In city after city, strikers and local citizens allied in open war against railroad capitalists; in Pittsburgh, the properties of the hated Pennsylvania Railroad were put to the torch, igniting a conflagration that illuminated the sky for miles around. As the strike spread from line to line, city to city, and region to region, it grew into the most massive and destructive industrial conflict in the late nineteenth-century industrial world.

Their scale and intensity made the 1877 strikes too turbulent for local and sometimes even state power to control. Everywhere respectable middle-class citizens bewailed the collapse of "law and order." Even state militia, dispatched to protect railroad property, proved unequal to the occasion. What the militia commander found to be true of his men at Martinsburg was the case elsewhere. "It is impossible for me to do anything with my company. Most of them are railroad men and they will not respond." In other states, militia also proved too undisciplined, and thus succeeded only in escalating the level of violence.

When the power of the states proved inadequate to keep the trains running and local communities orderly, railroad leaders turned to Washington. A series of cables and reports informed federal authorities about the existence of anarchy and insurrection beyond the power of state governments to control. Concerned most with the violent consequences of the railroad dispute and least with its causes, President Rutherford B. Hayes issued a proclamation declaring a state of emergency and insurrection, and then dispatched federal troops to Martinsburg, Baltimore, and Pittsburgh, among other places, to preserve the peace. The trains rolled again, and once more law and order was maintained at the expense of a group of strikers.

By the close of the 1870s, then, a pattern of conflict had been established in anthracite coal, in smaller industrial cities, and on the nation's railroads that would repeat itself regularly in the next two decades. At the start of a strike workers enjoyed a commanding position locally. Community merchants, professionals, and editors backed their working-class neighbors and customers in struggles against outside capitalists. Frequently local law enforcement officials elected by working-class votes or themselves union members assisted strikers in keeping scabs out. Stymied locally, employers would resort to external sources of power. State militia might be dispatched by a governor to a strike-torn community to preserve law and order, which often meant simply the protection of strikebreakers. Where militia proved inadequate to the task at hand, industrialists sometimes obtained federal troops, as happened during the railroad strikes and riots of 1877.

Between 1877 and the next sharp outbreak of working-class violence in 1886, the balance of power between workers and their employers had tipped in favor of the industrialists. Businessmen were proving more adept than laborers at either organizing themselves into associations that had power to influence the marketplace or smashing and swallowing their business competitors. As a result, businesses grew in size and capital resources. Less subject to pressure from competitors and more able to endure short-term financial losses, many firms were in a stronger position to discipline their workers and to risk industrial warfare. In addition, many firms now operated more than a single plant; thus a strike at one factory could be defeated by shifting production to another plant. Technological innovation also undercut the strength and security of workers. Formerly secure craftsmen in the iron and farm machinery industries suddenly found their skills superfluous, as new machines more efficiently performed their old jobs. Such was especially the case in the steel industry where the new techniques of production reduced the need for the craft skills so vital in the older iron industry. The impact of technological innovation was lucidly illustrated at McCormick Harvester, where in 1885 skilled molders had won a strike. Only a year later, however, McCormick introduced pneumatic molders in his Chicago plant and, though the new machines were not yet as efficient or productive as the old craftsmen, they could be run by unskilled workers when the molders struck. Thus in 1886, unlike 1885, when the molders walked out, production continued until the strikers surrendered. Also in 1886, unlike 1885, McCormick made sure to establish good relations with the Chicago police and city administration before risking a strike.

The growing economic power of employers and their alliance with government bred frustration among some militant workers and engendered a sense of desperation. Past events had already seen frustration and desperation explode in violence. In the 1880s militant workers and radical agitators more often resorted to the rhetoric of violence, nowhere more so than in the city of Chicago, where the spectre of unleashed anarchism set the middle and upper classes on edge. By 1886 Chicago had become the American center for radical and anarchist activities. There German immigrant workers belonged to rifle and marching clubs that appeared as revolutionary cells to worried middle-class citizens. And there in May 1886, in the aftermath of the molders' defeat at McCormick, police and strikers had clashed, causing the death of two workers and the wounding of several more. There, frustration and desperation were reaching a peak.

Shocked by the action of Chicago's police, August Spies, an anarchist and agitator among the city's workers, called for a protest meeting in Haymarket Square on the evening of May 4. Rumors of potential violence and even insurrection quickly spread, and a tense city awaited the evening of the fourth. The Haymarket protest meeting proved anticlimatic. A light drizzle dampened enthusiasm, a small crowd turned out, and the oratory for the most part was uninspiring. The anarchist speakers, instead of stirring their auditors to the barricades, seemed to inspire tranquillity. Yet, just before the meeting adjourned a squad of special police in attendance unexpectedly charged the crowd. Even more unexpectedly, a bomb was tossed into the melee. What until then had been an uneventful evening became a violent maelstrom, with the bomb killing police and civilians alike and the aroused police retaliating savagely against a defenseless and fleeing crowd.

As tragically as the meeting had ended, its aftermath was worse. One bomb, apparently thrown without reason and without explanation, convinced Chicago authorities and the city's middle and upper classes that insurrectionary violence was imminent. In order to thwart a potential revolutionary conspiracy, the police instituted a fine-mesh dragnet. Trade unionists, aliens, and vagrants were picked up wholesale, until the police satisfied themselves that they had in custody eight prime conspirators. These eight, who included August Spies and Albert Parsons, became the Molly Maguires of the 1880s. What passed for public opinion in Chicago and elsewhere in the nation assumed that all anarchists preached the "propaganda of the deed" (a concept that extolled acts of individual violence), that the bomb thrown at Haymarket Square represented such a deed, and that therefore the eight accused anarchists had either participated in throwing the bomb or had organized the conspiracy that caused it to be thrown. Police officials, city authorities, newspapers, magazines, and clergy did nothing to curb such notions; indeed, they contributed to the conspiracy image. Brought before a biased judge, indicted on loosely drawn conspiracy charges, tried in an inflamed community, faced with rigged evidence, and never confronted by the actual bomb thrower, the eight were convicted, with seven sentenced to be hanged. After all judicial appeals in the case failed, and one man committed suicide in jail, four unrepentant Haymarket martyrs, Spies and Parsons among them, were hanged on November 11, 1887. The remaining three were pardoned in 1894 in a courageous act by Illinois governor John Peter Altgeld.

Aside from taking the lives of five working-class radicals, Haymarket initiated the first nationwide Red Scare. A propaganda campaign of national proportions linked trade unionism with anarchy and anarchy with murder, thereby transforming all trade unionists into potential criminals. The antilabor, antiradical scenario written locally during the Molly Maguire trials reached a national audience with equally dire results for militant workers and radical agitators.

So completely did Haymarket absorb national attention and stir public anxiety that an equally violent industrial conflict in the year 1886 passed almost unnoticed—and in Chicago's backyard at that. The same month that the bomb was thrown in Chicago, strikers and militia clashed in Bay View, Wisconsin, an industrial suburb of Milwaukee, where Polish immigrant iron workers, supported by fellow Poles in the immigrant community, including priests, used crowd action to close local iron foundries. It took state militia willing to use their arms and to shoot over a score of strikers, more than ten fatally, to break the strike. Haymarket and Bay View repeated the recent past and presaged the near future.

As the power of large industrialists increased, so, too, did their desire to be rid of troublesome trade unions. And power could make wishes come true, as workers in the steel industry discovered. For a time in the 1870s and 1880s the Amalgamated Association of Iron and Steel Workers had been the most powerful craft union in the nation. Secure in the iron industry and its subsidiary trades, members of the Amalgamated could only watch in dismay as steel production grew more important and as the giant of the steel industry, Andrew Carnegie, proved his ability to produce uninterruptedly without union agreements. The union was unable to advance in steel because of the industry's technological innovations, and thus it struggled to retain whatever precarious footholds it had. The Amalgamated's intention of holding on in steel conflicted, however, with the steel masters' drive for economy and absolute control of work processes. Where the union still maintained power, the steel makers, Carnegie most notably, intended to end its influence.

When Carnegie acquired as part of his growing empire the Homestead, Pennsylvania plant in which a local of the Amalgamated functioned effectively and limited the mill super-intendent's prerogatives, it was only a matter of time before union and employer clashed. Much has been written about the violent conflict that erupted in Homestead in 1892. The causes of the conflict, its events, and its resolution are all clear enough and not in dispute.

What is most interesting about Homestead, then, is not its uniqueness but its perfect fit into the pattern of late nineteenth-century industrial conflict. Carnegie and his lieutenant in the dispute, Henry Clay Frick, agreed about goals but split over tactics. Carnegie, the humanitarian, preferred to starve union members into submission; Frick, the personification of the profit-conscious capitalist, preferred to fortify the plant, hire Pinkertons as Praetorian Guards, and use strikebreakers to smash the union without the loss of time, production, or profits. Frick's approach prevailed. The battle of Homestead followed on July 6, 1892, when armed strikers and fellow citizens of the community gathered on the bank of the Monongahela River to meet two barges of incoming Pinkertons. In the ensuing gun battle, one Pinkerton was killed, eleven were injured, and the whole lot surrendered abjectly to the triumphant union men. For the next four days, the workers of Homestead and their local supporters fully controlled the town and maintained peace and quiet. But on July 10, the governor of Pennsylvania, in response to pleas from Frick to protect private property and preserve law and order, ordered in the state militia. Under the protection of militia, strikebreakers went to work and belching mill chimneys signified the end of the Amalgamated in Homestead. When in November 1892 the union surrendered completely, Carnegie breathed a sigh of relief. "Life is worth living again," he cabled from Italy. "First happy morning since July...congratulate all around—improve works—go ahead—clear track." Not long afterwards, a traveler visited Homestead to observe conditions among the working class. "The managers represented 'Triumphant Democracy'[¹]," noted the visitor, "but nearly all that I saw while with the men might be described under the title of 'Feudalism Restored.'"

By the end of 1892 the lessons drawn by workers from two decades of industrial conflict were sufficiently clear. In most cases, by then, labor lacked the power to challenge concentrated capital. Where workers had the short-term ability to stalemate their employers, the state usually intervened and tipped the scales in favor of capital. Ideally, workers and their leaders preferred to avoid open battle. But the choice was not always theirs alone. Where employers took the offensive and sought to drive out unions, workers had no choice but to fight back. Where desperation and anger among the rank and file or the unorganized became too strong, labor leaders could not halt the struggle. Desperation, anger, and spontaneity would mark the last great conflict of the century—the Pullman Boycott of 1894— and write a fitting end to the nation's "time of chaos."

The story of the strike that pitted George Pullman and the major railroads of the Midwest against Eugene V. Debs and the American Railway Union (ARU) has been told many times. However dramatic and significant the Pullman Boycott was, its details need not concern us. Much more important is what the conflict revealed about the respective strength and political power of workers and employers. As we have already noted, in the years after the Civil War, the relative power of industrialists grew compared to that of their employees. While workers remained divided by craft, nationality, and race, employers united through mergers and trade associations. The first of the large modern business corporations in American society, railroads had long suffered from overcapitalization and excessive

¹The title of a book written by Carnegie.

competition, afflictions railroad managers sought to cure by means of informal and formal alliances. Not infrequently the railroad associations used their concentrated power to thwart the aims of the railroad brotherhoods, the industry's trade unions. It was to combat the united strength of management and end the divisions among the separate craft unions in the industry that Debs in 1893 founded the ARU, an organization that opened its doors to all (white) railroad workers regardless of skill. Shortly after its establishment, members of the ARU struck the Great Northern Railway and won a notable victory, proving Debs's brand of industrial unionism the apparent answer to corporate concentration.

Elated by its initial success, the ARU almost immediately found itself entangled in a conflict it neither expected nor sought. When George Pullman's workers pleaded with an ARU convention for assistance after repeated attempts to arbitrate their grievances had been rejected, Debs could not forestall his own union's delegates from a demonstration of working-class solidarity. The ARU voted to authorize its members to boycott all railroads using Pullman cars until the company bargained fairly with its workers. With a great show of labor solidarity, ARU members and their sympathizers brought most railroad traffic in the Midwest to a halt. But this initial union success was only a prelude to the then well-established process of managerial response.

As had happened in the past and would occur again in the future, railroad executives turned to public authorities to get their trains moving. Receiving less than total support from Governor Altgeld of Illinois, the nerve center of the boycott, the executives looked to Washington. There they found welcome support. President Grover Cleveland and Attorney General Richard Olney, a former railroad corporation attorney, threw the full resources of the federal government against the strikers. Cleveland announced that "if it takes every dollar in the treasury and every soldier in the United States to deliver a postal card in Chicago that postal card should be delivered," although strikers had promised not to interfere with the mail. To see that the card would indeed be delivered, Olney went to court and obtained injunctions outlawing the boycott, and Cleveland enforced the court orders. Against the full force of federal power, the strikers had little recourse. Debs himself was arrested and charged with criminal and civil contempt, ultimately to be convicted and sentenced to jail for the latter offense, a decision sustained in 1895 by the Supreme Court. Two federal statutes originally enacted to curb unpopular business practices—the Interstate Commerce Commission Act and Sherman Anti-Trust Act—provided the basis for the government's case against Debs and the ARU. Cleveland thus proved his courageous commitment to *laissez-faire,* and in so doing taught Debs the lesson that would transform him into a militant socialist.

This sordid history of industrial conflict, stained as it is by a trail of blood, makes one question standard assumptions concerning the American social order. It has been asserted with some validity that most Americans function within a common, or shared, value system, what Louis Hartz has labeled the Lockean consensus. This Lockean, or middle-class, consensus includes American workers who aspire only to the bourgeois goals of family, home, and business. In this version of our social structure, workers are distinguished from their employers *not* by values, behavior, and goals, but rather by the quantity of dollars possessed, the size of the home owned, and the amount of success achieved in the same race for business empire.

On the one hand, then, we have a value system shared by workers and employers alike. Yet, on the other hand, we encounter a history of violence and social conflict flowing steadily from the disorders associated with the depression of 1873–1877 to the Pullman strike. How can one explain the simultaneous existence of consensus and conflict? Is it a paradox which defies explanation? Or is there a possible answer?

First, it should be noted that most discussions of consensus in American history proceed at an exceedingly high level of abstraction. They tend to reflect how "ideal types" abstracted from the dense and real world of work and life would react in "ideal" circumstances. But most men and women live in a real world, a world of simple, everyday happenings, small pleasures and recurrent sufferings, which shape their attitudes as much as abstract principles. In the abstract, workers and employers might both worship the myth of the common man and his unfettered freedom to rise in society as symbolized by Abraham Lincoln. But what is one to make of the Lincoln myth in light of the realities of corporate concentration? Both workers and industrialists might subscribe to the importance of home ownership. But what is one to make of Carnegie's multimillion-dollar Fifth Avenue mansion compared to the two-room shack of a coal miner? Workers, as well as employers, might boast about America's democratic-republican heritage, its exceptionalism as a real "people's republic." But did democratic-republicanism carry precisely the same implications for both social classes? Certainly it seems likely that workers and industrialists might draw different meanings about the realities of the American political order from the facts of industrial conflict. That some workers did so is indicated in the following statement by a Pennsylvania coal miner:

The working people of this country suddenly find that their boasted Republicanism is not able to save them from the miseries which they sought to escape. They find monopolies as strong as government itself. They find capital as rigid as absolute monarchy. They find their so-called independence a myth, and that their subjection to power is as complete as when their forefathers were a part and parcel of the baronial estate.

The sort of republicanism exhibited by the coal miner's statement stressed the connections between hard labor and virtue. It praised work as the creator of human progress and happiness, labor as noble and holy. It defined capital as the product of past labor, not its ineluctable antithesis. Workers deserved the fruits of their labor (a just wage) and those who saved and invested wisely made other workers more fruitful and prosperous. "A republican society," one historian has written, "guaranteed the equal opportunity to labor, guaranteed to each the fruits of his toil, insured that no arbitrary social distinctions offered special privileges to some, but gave equal rights to all." It meant that workers should have the opportunity in life to achieve a competence—that is, a steady job, a home of one's own, and a secure old age. For some it might even encompass accumulation great enough to be ranked as a legitimate capitalist, one who through hard work and thrift in an open, competitive society fostered virtue and happiness among fellow republican citizens.

In the late nineteenth century, then, the vast majority of Americans shared a commitment to republican principles of state and society, to the ennobling experience of hard labor, and to a mutuality of interest between capital and labor. But even in a system in which people agreed on the fundamentals, as David Brody has written, "power and interest can be issues of deadly conflict," as indeed they were in the Gilded Age and after.

At the same time that workers worshipped principles in common with their employer, industrialists and their allies rewrote the rules of the game. They, not the workers, transformed the established structure of the local community and its traditional values. Employers substituted impersonal, bureau-cratic procedures for the face-to-face relationships that had once governed work in the nation's "island communities." Employers destroyed competitors or combined with them to capture the marketplace at which citizens worshipped free and open competi-tion. When local communities fought back against the new industrialists, employers enlisted the power of state and federal governments to discipline society's archaic "island communities." Industrialists succeeded, not because their values were at first superior or generally sanctioned, but because they were among the first Americans to learn that the problems of an industrial society, in the words of Sigmund Diamond (*The Nation Transformed* [1963]), "escaped individual solutions." As em-ployers increased their economic power, they also won many hitherto hostile communities to their side. Whereas in the 1870s industrialists had often been ostracized and opposed as "alien" influences, by the 1890s it was workers who began to find themselves isolated from previous sources of community support. Employers, not local laborers, had gained the ideological sympathy of community merchants and professionals.

Not only did industrialists learn the basic lesson of organization first; they also practiced organizational rationalization more successfully. "The attempt of persons to understand the forces remaking their world, and by organization, to control them," observes Diamond, "constitutes the major motif of the social history of the late nineteenth century."

THE LABOR MOVEMENT: FROM NLU TO AFL

Labor history proved no exception to Diamond's generalization, nor did workers ignore the example set by their employers. When workers discovered their nonlaboring former community allies increasingly turning to the employers' side in industrial conflicts, workingmen had no recourse but to rely on their own power. This meant that American workers would create, just as their employers had, organizations better able to defend their own place in the society and economy. By the end of the 1890s it was clear that security for the industrial worker lay in pooling strength with other laborers in national trade unions that united formerly autonomous local crafts. For only stable national organizations with reliable sources of revenue and substantial treasuries could survive strikes against powerful employers.

By the end of the Civil War the nation had had a long history of labor organization. Like so much else in American society, the vast majority of working-class organizations in the 1870s were locally rooted. From the founding of the first craft unions of printers, shoemakers, and carpenters in the 1790s, centrifugal forces had prevailed. Local unions of various crafts served as the working-class counterparts to the larger "island communities" that dotted the landscape. But just as "island communities" were rendered archaic by the nationalizing effects of transportation and communication innovations, local trade unions were powerless against regionally or nationally based employers. The history of labor organization in the late nineteenth century is thus the tale of various attempts to build working-class economic institutions able to struggle against national business corporations. It is also the history of the question of whether workers should organize to destroy the existing economic order or to function more successfully within it.

The older interpretation of American labor history originated by John R. Commons, Selig Perlman, and their many disciples fits the working-class organizations of the Reconstruction era into a neat and durable pattern. In that pattern, the trade unions represented the workers' natural and spontaneous response to their status as dependent employees. As organizations conceived, established, and administered by the workers themselves, the trade unions served the limited aims pursued by laborers, the most important of which was the worker's property right in his job. Trade unions were essentially *economic* organizations in harmony with working-class values and prepared to accommodate to the existing socioeconomic order. All other organizations, whether or not they claimed to be labor associations, were, according to the model proposed by Commons and Perlman, utopian reform bodies conceived and led by middle-class reformers and radical intellectuals. These reform associations moreover continuously misled workers.

According to this interpretation the thirty-two national trade unions which had come into existence by 1870, particularly the largest and most successful among them—the Iron Molders' International Union, the International Typographical Union, and the Knights of St. Crispin (shoemakers)—adequately served the needs of American workers and truly reflected their values and goals. Dedicated to winning higher wages, shorter hours, and the closed shop (job security) through collective bargaining, these organizations were on the right track. Unlike the trade unions, however, the various local labor parties, eight-hour leagues, and even the National Labor Union (NLU), which admitted trade unions and reform associations alike, sought the impossible: a noncapitalist, utopian society in which all men and women would be equal.

Commons's model has been consistently applied to scholarly treatments of the NLU. Founded at Baltimore in 1866, the NLU sought to give workers a national voice and also come to grips with some of the more challenging issues of the day—women's rights, the place of the black worker, the eight-hour day, and monetary reform. But, according to such historians as Norman Ware and Gerald Grob, as the NLU became increasingly involved in social-reform issues irrelevant to the needs of workers, the trade unions drifted away. By the time the NLU endorsed an independent national Labor Reform party in 1872, the organization had been, Norman Ware observes "taken over by labor leaders without organizations, politicians without parties, women without husbands, and cranks, visionaries, and agitators without jobs." Until American workers learned the irrelevance of reformism, middle-class panaceas, and intellectual blueprints for utopia, they were doomed, it seemed, to repeat the failure of the NLU.

More recently, however, the historian David Montgomery has provided a different interpretation of the labor movements of the immediate post–Civil War years. Stressing the commitment of American workers to republican social and political principles and their activities as all-around citizens, not purely economic men and women, he describes workers creating a variety of organizations in order to transcend the formal legal equality established by the Radical Republicans' political reforms, an equality which left the working class subordinate to its employers. Whether through trade unions, reform associations, labor parties, or the Marxist International Workingmen's Association, American workers pursued the social and economic power which would give meaning to legal equality. These workers would have understood Anatole France's famous aphorism that the law in its majestic impartiality forbids rich and poor alike from sleeping under bridges or on park benches.

Rewriting previous versions of American labor history, Montgomery proves that reform associations, labor parties, trades unions, and even the International Workingmen's Association, drew from the same constituency. In most cases, active and successful trade unionists led all four types of organization. Moreover the organizations differed in structure and function, not in objectives. Trade unions, as institutions designed to bargain with employers, limited membership solely to wage workers. Reform associations and labor parties, which were primarily educational and agitational, opened membership to all. And the NLU from its creation was largely a political institution whose objective was to provide workers with lobbying influence in Washington. William Sylvis, the most successful trade-union official of his day (president of the Molders' Union), also served as chief executive officer of the NLU until his untimely death in 1869. The most popular and intelligent radical labor reformer of the era, Ira Steward, was not a middle-class crank or intellectual, but rather a skilled machinist. Steward's crusade to win an eight-hour day was, as Montgomery indicates, *not* an idle panacea but part of a well-conceived program for the total renovation of society. It must also be remembered that at this stage in American history neither workers nor their union leaders necessarily accepted the triumph of industrial capitalism as inevitable or irrevocable. When industrial capitalism was in its infancy, alternatives seemed possible and so Sylvis could write to Karl Marx in 1868 concerning the First International: "Our cause is a common one... Go ahead in the good work that you have undertaken, until the most glorious success crowns your efforts... monied power is fast eating up the substance of the people. We have made war upon it, and we mean to win it. If we can we will win through the ballot box; if not, we will resort to sterner means. A little bloodletting is sometimes necessary in desperate cases."

Both practical and utopian, moderate and radical, economic and political, the working-class movement that emerged during the Civil War and its aftermath offered real promise for substantial change in the American social structure. Rather than being a simple throwback to the antimonopolism and middle-class reformism of the Jacksonian labor movement, the postbellum movement represented, as Montgomery establishes, a multifaceted attempt to render the emergent industrial society more egalitarian and humane. Also, as John O. H. P. Hall demonstrated, the activities of the Knights of St. Crispin, the largest single trade union of the period with some 50,000 members, reflected "signs of a group well advanced in learning how to defend the workers' status in industry."

The business cycle, however, sealed the fate of the labor movement. A severe economic depression which struck in 1873 and lasted until 1878 tore up the shallow roots of the young working-class movement. Already beset by internal difficulties and opposition from some of the more conservative trade-union interests, a gravely weakened NLU collapsed with the economy. The more moderate and pragmatic trade unions fared no better. As unemployment spread, jobless workers could not afford union dues. Never affluent, most trade unions became bankrupted. Battered by declining membership and falling income, the trade unions suffered from an employer antilabor offensive, which cut wages and union bargaining power. Workers forced to choose between jobs without a union, or a union without work, made the logical choice. Once again, as had happened earlier in 1837-1843, a promising working-class movement was destroyed by depression.

When militant and popular working-class organization next appeared on the American scene in the 1880s, an internecine battle tore labor's ranks, and its resolution determined the future structure and direction of the American labor movement. The bitter struggle which involved members of both the Noble and Holy Order of the Knights of Labor and the American Federation of Labor in the late 1880s resulted in a triumph for the trade union interests, which numerous historians have celebrated as a victory for the American worker.

To understand why the labor battle terminated as it did, we must comprehend first why, during the 1880s, the Knights of Labor was the more powerful and popular organization; what it symbolized at its zenith; and why it ultimately failed. Then we should examine what the AFL offered as an alternative to the Knights' program for workers, and why the Federation of Labor survived.

Briefly, the Knights originated in 1869 as a craft union of Philadelphia garment cutters, which copied the rituals and secrecy of the then popular fraternal societies. Before 1873 the Knights scarcely penetrated beyond the Philadelphia-Camden, New Jersey area. But unlike most other labor associations which collapsed in the depression of 1873, the Knights, partially as a result of the order's secrecy, survived. Then, when the return of prosperity in 1878 revived among workers the urge for organization, the Knights benefited.

At this point in its history, observes Norman Ware, the Knights "had no philosophy, no reforms, no political ambitions, no strange and ambitious titles. It was as pure and simple as the national trade unions and differed from them only in its ambition to include all trades and in its secrecy which was not unknown among them." But in 1878 at a convention held in Pennsylvania the Knights went public and national, and, in Ware's words, "accepted the tradition of the older national bodies, dressed themselves in preambles, platforms and titles, and launched upon the country, in theory if not in fact, another reform society." Yet neither Ware nor any other scholar offers a satisfactory explanation of the transformation of the Knights from a working-class economic organization to a middle-class reform society. Indeed, one is left asking, did such a mutation actually occur?

As we have noted previously, a substantial reservoir of working-class discontent had built up and at times threatened to overflow. The Knights capitalized on that discontent. Under the leadership of Terence V. Powderly, a former machinist, trade unionist, popular orator, and mayor of Scranton, Pennsylvania, the Knights dropped all secrecy in 1881 and opened its doors to all "producers," excluding from membership only bankers, lawyers, liquor dealers, speculators, and stock brokers. In that sense, the Knights, in theory, were a paradigm of a nation of island communities, in which all "respectable" members belonged to a common social brotherhood that cut across lines of occupation, wealth, nationality, religion, race, and sex. It also personified the republican ideology of the era, which stressed the virtue of labor, equality of opportunity, and community action. Scarcely limited in those it sought to organize, the Knights' objectives also were equally grandiose. Its 1884 General Assembly resolved: "Our order contemplates a radical change in the existing industrial system, and labors to bring about that change.... The attitude of our order to the existing industrial system is necessarily one of war." Note that this resolution does *not* declare war against industrialism, but only against the existing system. Also bear in mind that to achieve its ultimate objective of a new social order the Knights necessarily had to recruit a wide membership. A new, perhaps utopian, society would not, and could not, come about as a result of action by separate craft unions committed to protecting and advancing the position of their members within individual trades or industries. Solidarity was thus one of Powderly's fundamental beliefs and the principle underlying the Knights' ideal "that an injury to one is the concern of all." If the majority of Americans could indeed be organized by the Knights and subsequently educated to see the need for a different social order, then that same majority through economic cooperation and political action might build its new society. Hence, the Knights, like the NLU, was also an educational and agitational institution that transcended the functions of separate trade unions. Within the Knights, however, trade unions existed and functioned effectively as long as they respected the organization's basic principles and ultimate objectives.

The statistical evidence that we now have concerning the membership of the Knights suggests that few nonwage-earners belonged. True, especially in smaller cities, some small merchants and professionals as well as farmers from the surrounding countryside joined, but they were never more than a tiny minority. In its early years, more skilled, autonomous workers, like the founders of the original local of Philadelphia garment cutters, formed most local assemblies of Knights. Subsequently, especially after the Knights began to win strikes in 1885, less skilled workers, attracted by the organization's stress on solidarity, began to enroll in large numbers. So, too, did women workers who were welcomed more warmly by the Knights than by more conventional trade unionists. Finally, much evidence demonstrates that the overwhelming majority of the organization's officers were working-class in origin, not the children of failed middle-class parents nor themselves bourgeois reformers.

For most of its early history, however, the Knights remained insignificant. Then, suddenly, in 1885-1886 the organization burst into national prominence, standing at the center of what labor historians have customarily referred to as "the Great Upheaval of 1886." "Never in all history," wrote an editorialist in 1886, "has there been such a spectacle as the march of the Order of the Knights of Labor.... It is an organization in whose hands now rest the destinies of the republic.... It has demonstrated the overmastering power of a national combination among working-men." What occasioned such great expectations? Most simply, the Knights benefited from a fortuitous labor victory over Jay Gould's southwestern railroad lines in 1885 and a simultaneous spurt in growth, which by the spring of 1886 raised membership to an estimated 750,000.

The Knights grew so rapidly because it offered something for everyone. Its principle of solidarity, the motto "an injury to one is the concern of all," drew no distinctions among working people on the basis of skill, nationality, race, or gender. Its ambiguous principles enabled some to believe that it supported socialist revolution and others to see in it a repository of republican virtues. Some workers gravitated toward it as a militant fighting organization and others because it stood for a harmonious, nonconflictual social order. Yet others were attracted by its local political activities (Grand Master Workman Terence Powderly had himself served as labor party mayor of Scranton, Pennsylvania), or its commitment to temperance (Powderly was also a teetotaler), or its religiosity, or, in some cases, even its apparent feminism. To all these people, the Knights was proof that through organization workers could shape their destiny.

In a real sense, the rapid growth of the Knights proved its undoing. Hothouse expansion brought internal and external difficulties. Internally, Powderly was an excellent educator, speaker, and polemicist, but an inept administrator. In fact, the Knights lacked the administrative apparatus and experienced officials to manage its rapid membership increase. For a time in 1886, Powderly ordered organizers to stop enrolling members and issuing new charters. Externally, the organization's growth and strike victories occasioned an employer counterattack, which culminated in the post-Haymarket "red scare." By the end of 1886, Jay Gould had defeated the Knights in a second strike on his Southwestern lines, Chicago meatpackers had rescinded benefits just granted to members of local assemblies, and employers everywhere had goaded workers into strikes which the national organization could do little to assist.

The combination of internal and external pressures proved too much for Powderly and his associates to handle successfully. In the face of adversity, Powderly retreated. Instead of defending the eight Haymarket martyrs and the principle of labor solidarity, he condemned them. Rather than encouraging the local political activities in which Knights increasingly participated in 1886, Powderly demanded that members keep partisan politics out of the organization. When striking Knights beseeched the national office for material aid or moral support, he counselled mediation and conciliation. Instead of defending workers' interests in the here and now, Powderly focused on the role of education in teaching people the benefits of mutuality and cooperation in a far distant future.

The Knights, as Powderly's actions reveal, realized the enormity of their task and the strength of their enemy. As Ware suggests, the Knights "tried to teach the American wage-earner that he was a wage-earner first and a bricklayer, carpenter, miner, shoemaker after; that he was a wage-earner first and a Catholic, Protestant, Jew, white, black, Democrat, Republican after. This meant that the Order was teaching something that was not so in the hope that sometime it would be."

Thus, in the end, the promise of the Knights exceeded its performance, its solidarity proved ephemeral, and its members drifted away. As early as 1886-1887, more militant members had clashed with Powderly over his equivocal actions and antipathy to strikes. They formed an internal opposition, which found a receptive audience among strikers and craft unionists (trade assemblies) whose interests Powderly neglected. When Powderly refused to relinquish power, his opponents left (some were expelled) and many joined with the craft unionists who in 1886 had formed the American Federation of Labor. By 1893, when Powderly was finally driven from office, the Knights had lost most of its following in the industrial heartland and had the bulk of its membership concentrated west of the Mississippi River in regions where the unions associated with the AFL were absent or weak. By then the leadership of the national labor movement had passed to the craft unions and to Samuel Gompers and P. J. McGuire of the AFL.

History tends to be written by and for the victorious. Such has been the case with the Knights of Labor and the AFL. The impression one receives from reading about the AFL is of a "progressive," "realistic," "successful" organization in accord with the aspirations of its members and serving their interests well. Everything the Knights of Labor was not—well-administered, sensibly led, and rationalistic in the Weberian sense—the AFL was.

Thus we have the policies and practices of the AFL and its affiliated trade unions hailed as the unvarying standard by which to judge *all* American labor organizations. What, then, we may ask, are the specific principles and practices associated with trade-union success? First and foremost was the AFL's acceptance of industrial capitalism, what may be termed the trade unions' bargain with American employers. In return for allowing unions to bargain for their members over matters of wages, conditions, and security, employers received from labor leaders a general commitment *not* to disturb the capitalist system and a specific promise to adhere to the labor contract, even when it conflicted with the broader principle of working-class solidarity. Second was the trade unions' rejection of partisan politics and their preference for purely economic action, what has often been labeled "business, or bread-and-butter, unionism." Third, trade unionists rejected the advice and leadership of intellectuals and middle-class reformers. These three principles and the corollary practices that flowed from them can be distilled into the essence of the American worker's ideology: in Selig Perlman's words, "job consciousness." All the trade unions' internal policies and their external relationships with employers had but one objective: to defend the integrity and security of the worker's job. The typical trade union, as portrayed by Perlman and most other labor economists (also many historians) limited membership, instituted stringent apprenticeship rules, attempted to ration job opportunities by controlling the pace of production, and negotiated closed shop contracts, which denied employment to nonunion members. The degree to which the union succeeded in achieving those goals determined its appeal to the rank and file and its survival.

But how well, in fact, did the AFL and its affiliated unions succeed in their proclaimed goals? Moreover, were the original principles and practices of the late nineteenth century's trade unions as clear, precise, and unchallenged as some scholars have perceived them? Let us begin by trying to answer the latter question.

Too many generalizations about the nature of late nineteenth-century trade unionism have been based on the example of such unions of the highly skilled as the International Typographical Union. In a trade in which technological change failed to eliminate the need for skilled printers—in fact, skilled hand compositors proved the most productive linotype, or machine operators—the union could through control of the labor market determine work practices. In this case, union apprenticeship regulations, membership eligibility standards, and work rules preserved the skilled printers' independence and autonomy on the job. They also raised wages, shortened hours, and guaranteed jobs.

But the reality of Gilded Age trade unions was more complex than the case of the printers suggests. Historically, perhaps the most successful of all trade unions has been the

United Brotherhood of Carpenters and Joiners. Yet the Carpenters in the 1880s and 1890s were torn between two versions of trade unionism. On the one hand, P. J. McGuire, the founder of the union and one of the era's great labor leaders, believed that a union's primary concerns should be educational and agitational, that the union should educate its members to the supreme importance of the working class in society and to the need for a noncapitalist, nonexploitative system. On the other hand, other officials in the Carpenter's Union, the so-called walking delegates or business agents, were concerned primarily with creating an institution that would be the workers' answer to employers' business corporations. These business agents struggled long and hard to make their type of "business unionism" dominant, and not until *after* 1900 would their victory become final. Most working carpenters appeared to be drawn toward both versions of trade unionism, for they persistently reelected McGuire to office and relished the material benefits provided them by the business unionism practiced by the walking delegates.

In the 1880s and 1890s such unions as the United Mine Workers, the Machinists, the Brewery Workers, and the Boot and Shoe Workers, among others, remained committed to Populist and socialist politics. The actual process of creating the "pure and simple, job conscious, business union" was long and slow. In short, what too many historians have done is to observe the national craft unions at their successful best in the Progressive years (1900–1916) and then to read the characteristics of success back into the formative years.

Almost the same can be said regarding versions of the AFL's success. When we turn from embellished portraits of the AFL's past to its reality, a different picture emerges. Instead of a lusty, potent, and secure trade-union giant, we glimpse a scared, uncertain, insecure infant. Founded originally in 1881 as the Federation of Organized Trade Unions of the U.S. and Canada, the AFL was almost stillborn. Resurrected in 1886 as the AFL by a group of trade unionists dissatisfied with the Knights of Labor, it bequeathed to its president, Gompers, an empty treasury and an eight-by-ten office equipped with a kitchen table, a child's writing desk, crates, and boxes. For four months Gompers went without salary, while the family of the president of the AFL had to borrow money to buy groceries. The number of national unions affiliated with the AFl did grow from thirteen to forty by 1892, but most of them were small and in parlous financial condition. Indeed, we lack accurate membership figures for the AFL of 1886-1893; in 1890, for example, reported membership fluctuated between 225,000 and 630,000. When depression struck in 1893 membership fluctuated more wildly, and statistics for the years 1893-1896 grew even more unreliable. In 1897, a decade after its birth and on the eve of its first period of substantial growth, the AFL counted 447,000 members, well below the Knights' peak membership in 1886. The AFL, unlike the Knights, might publicly endorse strikes, but, like the Knights, it lacked the financial resources to support actual strikers; militant as Gompers may have sounded in his rhetoric, in the event of a dispute, he usually counseled moderation and conciliation.

What of the national trade unions which were the principal source of power and authority in the labor movement? Their record, with few exceptions, in the late nineteenth century is scarcely more impressive. At the time of the AFL's founding, the Amalgamated Association of Iron, Steel, and Tin Workers was probably the nation's largest and most powerful trade union. Six years later, after Homestead, it was whipped and nearly impotent in the steel industry. The other trade unions, marginally more successful than the Amalgamated, staggered from crisis to crisis. Not one of them had recruited as much as one-third of the workers in its trade, and not one could have truthfully been said to maintain a secure existence. All together, the trade unions included fewer than 5 percent of American wage workers, and of those 5 percent many were on the fringes of the economy. The dominant sectors of the industrial world, especially the emerging mass-production industries, remained impenetrable to the trade unionists. Despite the trade unionists' customary bows to the principle of brotherhood and solidarity, union membership was in practice reserved for a privileged few. "Organized labor in

America," observed Friedrich Engels in 1892, "still occupies an aristocratic position and wherever possible leaves the ordinarily badly paid occupations to the immigrants, only a small portion of whom enter the aristocratic trade unions."

What success the AFl and its affiliates enjoyed, if success it can be called, consisted in surviving the depression of 1893-1897. Beyond that, no one observing the American scene in 1897 could have predicted a future for the AFL brighter than the past of the Knights of Labor. This should caution students of history that they must avoid at all costs reading subsequent historical developments back into a past that may have been far different. The paragraphs that follow should also warn students about assuming that values associated with contemporary Americans were necessarily those held dear by men and women in times past.

WORKERS AND POLITICS

Just as the Typographical Union's practices became synonymous with those of trade unions in general, and the character trade unions assumed in the Progressive era was read back into the Gilded Age, so, too, have several scholars, following the tradition originally set by Commons and Perlman, assumed that the AFL's approach to politics in the Progressive era was merely the continuation of a tradition set in the nineteenth century. That interpretation of labor and politics perceives the ideal trade unionist as an individual whose role as a trade unionist does not determine his behavior as a voter. The mature trade union movement consequently places politics and economics in two distinctly separate spheres of action which ideally should never impinge upon each other. Unions, as the instruments of job conscious workers, must avoid participation in partisan politics and do their utmost to keep politicians at arm's length.

But just as our picture of nineteenth-century trade unionism becomes distorted by viewing it through the lens of a subsequent labor movement, so, too, is the relationship between workers and politics mystified by confusing the labor movement of the 1920s with that of the period from 1870 to 1897. The remarkable feature about labor politics in the late nineteenth century is the consistency of organized labor's political role. From the NLU to the Knights of Labor to the AFL the leaders of those organizations concentrated on representing labor's interests in Washington through intensive lobbying. And from the era of Reconstruction to the age of Populism, workers and trade unionists at the local and state levels participated regularly in a variety of independent and third-party political campaigns. Yet, however much we know about the bare outlines of labor politics in the late nineteenth century, the bulk of its inner history is just becoming clear.

Before examining more closely the role of labor in politics, several general points must be kept in mind. In the United States, unlike most of Western Europe, the achievement of manhood suffrage and the emergence of trade unionism preceded the rise of political socialism. American workers did *not* gain the ballot as a result of trade-union campaigns or socialist crusades. Consequently by the late nineteenth century most American-born workers had had their political consciousness molded as Republicans or Democrats. Moreover the Civil War and its aftermath had tended to reinforce already intense party loyalties. The appeal of independent working-class politics, already undermined by preexisting party loyalties, was further vitiated by the existence of single-member constituencies, a device which crippled third-party candidacies, and the federal structure of government, which made successful campaigning expensive and time-consuming. Adding still further to labor's political weakness were the effects of mass immigration, ethnicity, and race, perhaps the most divisive influences among workers. It must be stressed that the American environment was as unconducive to working-class politics as it was to trade unionism.

Despite the barriers they had to cross, American workers seldom hesitated to enter the political arena, either independently or in alliance with other excluded interest groups. Labor politics, which originated on the local and state levels in the 1860s to obtain legislative regulation of hours and working conditions, evolved by 1872 and 1876 into the national Greenback-Labor party, which contested presidential elections. Not successful, to be sure, in presidential politics, Greenback-Laborites did, however, succeed during the depression of the 1870s in electing numerous municipal and state officials, as well as a handful of congressmen.

The next burst of working-class political action coincided with the "Great Upheaval" of 1886. In that year, Henry George, as labor-reform candidate for the mayor of New York, frightened the major parties and polled more votes than Theodore Roosevelt, the Republican party candidate. In Chicago and Cook County, a United Labor party polled 25,000 of 92,000 total votes and elected a state senator and seven assemblymen. Ninety miles to the north, the People's party of Milwaukee carried the county and elected the mayor, six assemblymen, and a congressman. Labor parties also won notable victories in Leadville, Colorado; Newark, New Jersey; Fort Worth, Texas; Lynn, Massachusetts; Norwalk, Connecticut; Kansas City, Kansas; Rutland, Vermont; and Richmond, Virginia. For reasons still to be explored, however, labor's political tide ebbed as rapidly as it had risen. By 1887 most of the previous year's successful labor parties were a shambles.

Recent studies suggest several possible explanations for the collapse of independent working-class political action. In an essay that appeared in 1964 Carl Degler suggested that the Republican party in the late nineteenth century cultivated support from urban industrial workers and that Republicanism was preeminently the politics of the city. Other historians, by closely examining political behavior in the Midwest and Northeast of the 1880s and 1890s, have hypothesized that ethnic and religious influences were more important than class and economic issues in determining the voting behavior of unorganized workers. They also argue that by the 1890s the Republican party of Mark Hanna and William McKinley consciously appealed to the ethnic and religious preferences of non-

Protestant immigrant workers, while restraining antilabor sectors of the party. Carefully deflating class issues, proclaiming itself the party of high wages secured through protective tariffs, and opposing prohibitionist and anti-Catholic tendencies, Hanna Republicanism attracted many industrial workers, especially in the industries and regions which received the highest tariff protection.

The decline of labor politics after the upheaval of 1886 and Republicanism's growing appeal to industrial workers should not, however, blind us to the persistence of radical working-class political action in the late nineteenth century. In this era socialism also appeared on the American scene. In fact, as we have seen, William Sylvis and the NLU had flirted with the Marxist International Workingmen's Association (IWA), an organization eventually buried in 1872 in Philadelphia. The year 1877 saw socialism reappear in the guise of the Socialist Labor Party, a narrow sectarian organization of German immigrants who conducted all their business in German and had very little contact with English-speaking workers. In the mid-1880s, the SLP began to recruit Jewish immigrant members in New York and Chicago, but they, too, were separated from the mass of American workers by a language barrier. Not until the 1890s was socialism Americanized under the dual influence of Edward Bellamy and Daniel DeLeon. But unfortunately for the future of socialism in America, DeLeon, the self-appointed dictator to the SLP, engaged in an unnecessary and self-defeating battle with Gompers and the trade-union leaders, a struggle that permanently embittered relationships between trade unionists and socialists and also split the minuscule American socialist movement. Reflecting on the American political scene as it appeared to him in 1892, Engels informed an American correspondent: "There is no place yet in America for a *third* party.... The divergence of interests even in the *same* class group is so great... that wholly different groups and interests are represented in each of the two big parties... and almost each particular section of the possessing class has its representatives in each of two parties.... Only when there is a generation of native-born workers that cannot expect *anything* from speculation *any more,* will we have solid foothold in America."

No sooner had Engels written off the prospects of third-party political action in the United States than events disputed his verdict. For a time in the 1890s, as depression, unemployment, and violent industrial conflict impelled labor toward political action, a nationwide farmer-labor alliance seemed a likely and potent political prospect. Many American farmers, feeling themselves helpless before the rigidity and impersonality of the international market and its price mechanisms, began to turn to independent politics in the 1880s, a movement which climaxed in the birth of the People's party (1892) and the Populist crusade. In the event, however, the political marriage between workers and farmers ended before it could be consummated.

Ever since the failure of farmer-labor politics in the 1890s, historians have sought a reason for the collapse of the coalition. Some have blamed agrarians for their capitalist cupidity; others have accused labor of serving as the regressive political factor. In the hyperbolic words of the historian Norman Pollack: "The A.F.L.'s failure to act guaranteed the actual downfall of Populism; the Federation through looking the other way killed the farmer-labor movement." Thus Pollack implants the notion that, in contradistinction to most Marxist and radical analyses of social action, farmers were radical and trade unionists conservative.

A comparable interpretation, not beholden to Marxist categories of analysis, has been proposed by Lawrence Goodwyn. He believes that economically exploited southern farmers in the late 1880s developed a "movement culture," a culture in conflict with the emerging dominant elitist, individualistic, materialistic, and capitalistic values of national society. Movement farmers, according to Goodwyn, were democratic, cooperative, idealistic, and nonexploitative. They built a radical movement—Populism—in a last-ditch effort to establish popular democracy. Urban-industrial workers, by contrast, never developed a "movement culture" of their own, one at odds with the conservative order. Thus Goodwyn, like Pollack, portrays agrarian Populists as radicals and urban workers as cultural conservatives.

To use such abstract and pejorative terms as radical and conservative functions in this case only to mystify the processes of history. That farmers and workers failed to form a successful radical political coalition in the 1890s is a fact of history. But to argue, that one group was radical and the other conservative is to distort the realities. Indeed, the main obstacle to unity was not the radicalism of one party and the conservatism of the other; rather it was the different material interests and objectives represented by farmers and workers. It is also too easy to magnify the real differences between farmer and labor groups out of all proportion and thus to lose sight of certain common political goals.

During the 1890s both farmers and workers suffered from depression, and as the two largest oppressed groups in society, they turned to politics to redress their grievances. The form that their protest assumed depended to a great extent on the social, economic, and political milieu in which they functioned. In the primary industrial area of the nation, east of the Mississippi and north of the Ohio rivers, where the vast majority of workers lived and organized labor had most influence, the People's party was almost nonexistent. There traditional party loyalties remained firmest, agrarians had either adjusted to industrialism or lost influence, and workers, the overwhelming majority of whom were unorganized, lacked a real alternative to the two established parties. In the cotton South and wheat West, the heartland of agrarian Populism, wage workers, a minority of the population, tended to cooperate with agrarian radicals and to join enthusiastically in Populist campaigns. Finally, in the mining states of the mountain West and also on the Pacific Coast, labor tended to be the dominant element in the Populist coalition. This was particularly true of the mountain states of Colorado, Idaho, Montana, and Nevada, where organized wage earners dominated the local Populist organizations and wooed agrarian interests.

Even in Wisconsin and parts of Illinois and Ohio (coal-mining counties), workers, not farmers, formed the core of Populism. What you see then, in effect, is no clear pattern of farmer-labor politics: in one case, the industrial Northeast, workers seemed uninvolved with Populism; in a second instance, farmers and workers united politically; and in a third case, organized workers controlled Populism but met some agrarian resistance. Above and beyond such regional complexity, however, towered a fundamental material split between workers and agrarians. Farmers saw their economic salvation in free silver, cheap money, and inflation; wage workers preferred cheap food, hard money, and high wages. Daniel DeLeon put the dilemma succinctly: "Populist farmers are to get free silver at sixteen to one, so that they may pay their debts with depreciated money and thus become capitalists; the Populist politicians will get the spoils of office, while the Populist wage workers will mop their foreheads and rub their empty stomachs with a glittering generality."

In the end, however, agrarian Populists and organized workers did unite politically: in the election of 1896, the People's party endorsed the candidacy of Democratic presidential nominee William Jennings Bryan; Gompers, despite professing loyalty to the AFL's proclaimed policy of nonpartisanship, in fact, worked for Bryan. Bryan, of course, lost to McKinley.

The reasons for the failure of the farmer-labor coalition in the Bryan campaign of 1896 are in certain respects clear. Engels in his 1892 letter noted a vital factor: "The small farmer and the petty bourgeois will hardly ever succeed in forming a strong party; they consist of elements that change too rapidly—the farmer is often a migratory farmer, farming two, three, and four farms in succession in different states and territories... but to make up for it they are a splendid element for politicians, who speculate on their discontent in order to sell them out to one of the big parties afterwards." A second factor at work in the 1890s was the substantial likelihood that most newer immigrant industrial workers either lacked the franchise or saw little reason to use it. Finally, and perhaps most important, organized labor had too few members to affect decisively the outcome of national elections. Gompers's realization and acceptance of these factors led him to prefer alliances with the established parties which, as we shall see in the next chapter, brought organized labor into a working relationship with the Democratic party. Socialists, aware of the same forces in American politics, decided for the time being to neglect agrarian reformers and instead to concentrate on building the urban-industrial wing of their party among wage workers and newer immigrants. The political experience of trade unionists and radicals during the depressed nineties would shape their policies and actions in the Progressive era to follow.

As the nineteenth century drew to its close most American workers were unable to act on the knowledge that the problems of industrial society "escaped individual solutions." Unwilling, or unable, to join labor organizations, most workers lacked the power to influence the conditions of work. If their families, ethnic associations, mutual-aid societies, and often churches provided workers the means to control life in their immediate neighborhoods, they remained powerless to shape decisively the national social and economic environment. The minuscule minority of organized workers also lacked power as substantial as that of corporate executives. Having learned the lesson of collective action and having acted on it, trade unionists still had failed to achieve the organizational rationalization, bureaucratic innovations, and market power won by their capitalist adversaries. Big business in America had successfully pioneered the emerging bureaucratic-technological society; workers, to their own grave disadvantage, remained caught between the island communities and personalism of a dying order and the emergence of a modern organizational society.

Industrial relations are essentially human relations...

JOHN D. ROCKEFELLER, JR.

I think capital should recognize organized and responsible labor just as labor should recognize organized and responsible capital.

GEORGE W. PERKINS

THREE

Time of Reform, 1897–1914

Historians have customarily characterized the first decade and a half of the new century as a "Progressive" era, a period when Americans struggled to reform their society. Attracted to Theodore Roosevelt and Woodrow Wilson, partial to the crusades led by a myriad of reformers, and sympathetic to a new breed of intellectuals who shattered values inherited from the nineteenth century, scholars have portrayed the years between 1900 and 1914 glowingly. It was a time when Progressive politicians and reformers tamed the "Robber Barons," cleaned up the cities, purified politics, and laid the foundations for the welfare state.

But the traditional portrait of Progressivism obfuscates the era's more significant elements of social change. Omitted from many histories, or perceived as objects, not subjects, are two vital participants in the era's reforms—big businessmen and industrial workers. The businessmen are too often portrayed as the victims of popular antipathy and governmental regulation; the workers are patronized as the wards of social reformers or the beneficiaries of government benevolence. That corporate leaders and ordinary laborers played a dynamic role in constructing a new social order is rarely noticed.

EMPLOYERS, WORKERS, AND PROGRESSIVISM

Fortunately, a large body of scholarship has revised for the better older interpretations of Progressivism. A many-faceted revisionism has replaced "liberal" optimism, complexity has triumphed over simplicity. No longer can we regard the era as one during which the people subdued the "special interests," the statesmen overwhelmed the "bosses," and altruistic reformers cleansed society's most noisome sores. Many historians have given a new look to Progressivism. More than that, some of them have questioned the very notion of a Progressive movement in a Progressive era. Instead of sharply distinguishing the first sixteen years of the twentieth century from the preceding three decades, these scholars have placed the Progressive period in the center of a historical continuum which runs from the creation of a modern industrial society in the aftermath of the Civil War to the establishment of a mass bureaucratic order in the wake of World War II.

This new scholarship has challenged the premise that reform resulted from the "people's" triumph over the "interests." Rather it indicates that many reforms originated in conflicts between competing special interest groups, and also how, notably at the urban level, reform meant the loss of popular political power and influence. Historians have also increasingly analyzed the manner in which professionalization and bureaucratization, not quixotic altruism, triggered the reform impulse. Finally, recent research demonstrates the extent to which business interests shaped the passage of national reform legislation. In sum, this "new history" suggests that the changes that occurred in American society between 1900 and 1916 owed much to the direct influence of corporate interests and the transformation of reformers from amateur philanthropists to trained, professional social workers or engineers. In most of this new scholarship, however, the role of organized and unorganized workers rarely comes into sharp focus. Working people remain bit players in the drama of reform.

Yet almost all historians agree that workers were among the major beneficiaries of the period's reform legislation. Still, they dispute the motives and causes for such reform. One school of interpretation suggests that middle-class reformers used the state coercively to compel businessmen to improve working conditions in order to avert violence or revolution from below. A second school asserts that it was the industrialists themselves who initiated reforms. These "corporate liberals" or "welfare capitalists" ameliorated working conditions, sponsored job-safety campaigns, provided their employees with medical care and pensions, favored positive state action, and even recognized responsible unions in order to thwart the growth of radical labor and political socialism. Finally, a third set of scholars asserts that the pressure of working-class voters and the political influence of their representatives contributed decisively to the passage of social-welfare reforms.

What emerges most clearly from the divergent interpretations of American history in the opening years of the twentieth century is the development of a bureaucratic-technological society. As Robert Wiebe stresses, the island communities, personal relations, and informal rules of nineteenth-century society left most Americans bewildered by a nation dominated by gigantic, modern industrial corporations which were governed by impersonal, formal managerial bureaucracies. To protect themselves against the inroads of technology and bureaucracy, Americans had to surrender the sovereignty of their island communities to larger, more impersonal instruments of political governance and to accept the institution of formal rules of life and behavior. Society, for example, could no longer allow workers to shift for themselves in an imaginary free marketplace, or be subject to the whims of their employers. Working-class life had to be regularized and routinized. And this was a matter about which social reformers, legislators, and industrialists concurred. Differences arose about the proper means to the regularization of working-class life but seldom about the ultimate end. This commitment from outside the ranks of American labor to the formalization of work rules proved to be one major motif of working-class existence in the Progressive era.

By the end of the nineteenth century, it had also become evident to many Americans that unregulated working conditions and the free market in urban real estate caused the exploitation of millions of workers and in turn provoked protest and violence from below. With stunning regularity, scholarly studies and popular journalistic exposés (of which Upton Sinclair's *The Jungle* [1904] proved the most sensational) demonstrated the mayhem inflicted on workers in American factories and the fetid conditions of existence in urban slums. As workers had proved unable to protect themselves and employers seemed unwilling to alter prevailing conditions, social reformers argued that the state should interpose itself between workers and employers, slum-dwellers and landlords, in order to protect the helpless from the powerful. Reformers found support for their position in recent discoveries made by practitioners of industrial medicine and sanitary engineering, as well as in the precedent of Bismarckian welfare legislation in Imperial Germany and the "New Liberalism" then being implemented in Britain. Why could not new forms of knowledge be used to render American factories and cities more amenable to human existence? Why should not the American state do at least as much to protect its working-class citizens as the governments of Germany and Great Britain?

The above questions led to positive action, and the United States fashioned its own version of Bismarckian reforms and

"New Liberalism," but with several important differences. First, American constitutional law, as it was interpreted and implemented in the early twentieth century, denied federal authorities a large role in the sphere of social welfare. Hence most reform measures had to be enacted at the state level, preventing the uniformity that prevailed in German and British welfare law. Furthermore, American welfare legislation tended to leave a larger scope for private insurance groups and voluntary associations than for government agencies, to administer the desired reforms. Some historians explain the privatism and voluntarism of American reform in terms of an exceptional American ideology shared by all social classes, which preferred private, associational social change to state originated and executed reform. But it might also be argued that American welfare legislation derived more from differences in the distribution of economic and political power than from formal ideology. American industrialists, unlike their British and German counterparts, never had to subdue noncapitalist or anticapitalist aristocrats who might ally with working-class radicals to put down bourgeois parvenus. This, too, may explain why so much American factory and welfare legislation remained unenforced. (In fact, although we know a great deal about what kind of reform legislation was passed and the politics of its enactment, we know less concerning its implementation.)

These distinctions notwithstanding, American state legislatures between 1900 and 1914 enacted a wide variety of welfare laws. Most industrial states passed employers' liability or workmen's compensation laws to protect laborers against industrial accidents; the same states tended to restrict the types of jobs at which women and children might labor and to regulate their hours of work; a few states even sought to establish minimum wages for women; legislatures prescribed rules governing sanitation and safety in industrial plants; and city councils as well as state bodies enacted more restrictive building and real estate codes.

But concentration on state and local efforts in the welfare field should not obscure the federal authorities' contributions to the regularization of work processes in areas where they felt free to act. Theodore Roosevelt, for example, instituted an employers' liability program for federal workers and intervened in the anthracite coal strike of 1902 differently from previous presidents; instead of using federal power to smash a strike, Roosevelt exercised his influence to win several concessions for the miners and their union. William Howard Taft, who on the federal bench had built a reputation as a notorious antilabor injunction judge, as president laid the basis for the establishment of the cabinet-level Department of Labor (1913) and the United States Commission on Industrial Relations, which between 1913 and 1915 investigated and condemned the nation's primitive industrial-relations practices. Finally, under Woodrow Wilson, federal contributions to workers' welfare reached their zenith. Eager to win the political support of Gompers, the AFL, and the nation's workers, Wilson appointed a former United Mine Workers official (William B. Wilson) as the first secretary of labor, cleared many other federal appointments with prominent labor leaders, and sponsored a host of reforms in national labor law. During the two Wilson administrations, organized labor gained a measure of relief from antitrust legislation under the Clayton Act; merchant seamen received protection of their rights in the La Follette Seamen's Act of 1915; railroad workers won an eight-hour day through the Adamson Act of 1916; and legislation, later to be declared unconstitutional by the Supreme Court, outlawed child labor.

The variety of welfare legislation enacted seems in retrospect remarkable; the causes and dynamics of its passage remain more obscure. Numerous books and essays detail almost endlessly the crusades for welfare led by a myriad of middle-class social reformers. The National Consumers' League, the Child Labor Committees, the settlement house workers of whom the most famous were Jane Addams, Lillian Wald, and Robert Woods, the American Association for the Advancement of Labor Legislation, and the Women's Trade Union League, among other such organizations, are the subject of innumerable monographs and scholarly articles. The means by which these organizations and their spokesmen translated concern for social welfare into political influence and legislative power, however, remains unclear. Also less than obvious is the precise sort of relationship middle-class reformers maintained with trade unionists and with the unorganized masses whom they sought to serve as trustees.

With a few striking exceptions, the middle-class reformers, despite the growing professionalization of social work and the use of medical and social sciences in the reform cause, operated in the tradition of *noblesse oblige*. They may have descended into the gutter to aid the less fortunate but in the process they made sure not to soil their clothes. The working-class beneficiaries of middle-class concern sensed this patronizing approach. As one young immigrant garment worker told a group of eminent New York City reformers in the aftermath of an industrial tragedy, workers had tried the reformers and found them wanting. "Too much blood has been spilled," she went on. "I know from my experience that it is up to the working people to save themselves."

But how could working people save themselves if they were politically divided and impotent as much historical research contends? Indeed, how and why was all the welfare legislation of the Progressive period enacted if reformers and unionists were often at odds and workers usually ineffective and inept in the realm of politics?

This last question brings us to the motivations of the legislators who actually passed the laws. What prompted them to enact welfare legislation? How responsive were they to reform societies and trade unions? How much was their legislation determined by principle and how much by political expediency? One interpretation asserts that the politicians of the period responded to welfare problems in Bismarckian fashion. Working in harmony with their capitalist masters, politicans enacted reforms primarily in order to ameliorate working-class discontent and stifle an emerging socialist movement. Dedication to the principles of capitalism and a paternalistic concern for the potentially volatile masses, in short, motivated political reform. But another school of historians contends that the era's most prominent and successful reform politicians responded to the needs and desires of their working-class constituents. Rather than supporting welfare legislation at the behest of large industrialists, the Robert Wagners, Charles Murphys, and Al Smiths understood and acted directly for their constituents. Of course, in their case, serving their constituents also meant thwarting more radical political alternatives, as socialism seemed more of a threat than Republicanism in their Democratic districts.

Whatever the motivations for social reform, its impact on the lives of most workers was probably less substantial than that of changes in technology and working conditions introduced by most large industrialists and many smaller ones. Just as the large corporations had previously rationalized their internal organizational structures and external market relationships, they now sought to regularize work processes and industrial relations within the plant. Nineteenth-century work practices were, as we observed in a previous chapter, based on a mélange of tradition, custom, artisan knowledge, and craft union rules, all of which limited the employer's effective power. Equally irksome to large industrialists concerned with continuity and efficiency of production were high labor turnover, excessive absenteeism, alcoholism, and avoidable industrial accidents. The giant corporations and their smaller imitators hit upon a double-barrelled approach to internal industrial relations. On the one hand, managers introduced "scientific" techniques into the production process, vitiating, in theory, the dead hand of custom and craftsman guesswork while enlarging managerial prerogatives and lowering the costs of production. On the other hand, companies experimented with a variety of employee reforms, which fell under the rubric "welfare capitalism," and were intended to diminish labor turnover, absenteeism, and accidents. For management the two approaches had a single, harmonious objective—the formation of a satisfied labor force that would function continuously entirely at managerial direction in the most efficient manner. For workers, as we shall see, the two approaches conflicted: welfare capitalism stimulated loyalty; scientific management repelled it.

Between 1880 and 1920, and with increasing rapidity after 1900, employers reshaped the environment of the factory and the flow of work. By improving illumination and ventilation, eliminating spatial obstacles to smooth production, maintaining better inventories of tools, and restricting the arbitrary authority of immediate shopfloor supervisors, employers introduced what the historian Daniel Nelson has called the "new factory system." In this system, staff rather than line managers used modern, rational managerial methods (the fruits of formal education and science) to hire workers, organize their labor, remunerate them, discipline them, and discharge them.

Although the new factory system had many component parts, one in particular caught the popular imagination and fueled controversy—Taylorism, or scientific management. Seldom ever introduced fully into practice and often actually opposed by employers, the form of scientific management associated with the name Frederick Winslow Taylor nevertheless represented one of the central tendencies operative in the reorganization of work.

What was Taylorism and why was it so controversial a system of work management? In theory, Taylor offered something to everyone. He promised employers greater productivity, higher profits, and a union-free environment. He offered workers higher wages and the single most efficient way of laboring. And he enticed consumers with the bait of better products at lower prices. All this would be achieved by putting the science of engineering into the service of humanity on the shop floor. Under Taylorism trained engineers would carefully observe workers on the job, gather and codify the great mass of traditional knowledge, which in the past was possessed entirely by workmen who acquired it through hit-and-miss experience and used it in the same way. Would not such a study by engineers inevitably lead to simpler jobs for workers, higher productivity per unit of labor, more wages for the workman, and reduced prices for the consumer? Admittedly, under scientific management, workers would lose a considerable amount of their already diminished on-the-job authority, but in return they would receive more money and, as Henry Ford observed: "... no man wants to be burdened with the care and responsibility of deciding things."

The logic underlying Taylorism was perhaps most clearly revealed in the meatpacking and automobile industries, where in the former case the disassembly line, and in the latter case the assembly line, mechanically set the pace of production. "Fordism," as Europeans called this system, made factory workers into automatons who, in return for high wages, surrendered all real control over actual work practices.

In practice, however, the rewards of Taylor's policies flowed largely to management. And there was little reason why they should not, given the unprotected economic position of most workers and the supercilious attitude toward workmen that Taylor shared with his generation of industrial engineers. What could workers really expect from a man who asserted, "I can say without the slightest hesitation, that the science of handling pig-iron is so great that the man who is fit to handle pig-iron and is sufficiently phlegmatic and stupid to choose this for his occupation is rarely able to comprehend the science of handling pig-iron...?" What happened, in fact, was that scientific management, wherever implemented, accelerated the pace of work, reduced the worker's remaining authority over his job, and provided no commensurate increase in material rewards. This explained both organized labor's opposition to scientific management and employers' desire to introduce Taylorism among unorganized workers.

Another aspect of managerial labor practices in the early twentieth century stressed the welfare of workers, responsibility to the community, and public relations. This approach was typified in the efforts of the National Civic Federation (NCF), founded in 1900, as an institution which would publicize and promote more rational systems of industrial relations. Administered by bureaucrats, the NCF included on its advisory board such great industrialists as August Belmont, Mark Hanna, and Elbert Gary; such trade union leaders as Sam Gompers and John Mitchell; and such eminent representatives of the public interest as Grover Cleveland, William Howard Taft, and Andrew Carnegie (recently retired as an active industrialist). According to its own printed propaganda, the Civic Federation encouraged the growth of responsible, conservative unions, which would in practice discipline workers for the benefit of their employers; it promoted the substitution of tripartite boards of mediation for old-fashioned strikes and lockouts; it publicized and assisted companies in introducing effective programs of plant safety; it stimulated employers to adopt such features of welfare capitalism as pension benefits and medical insurance; and it lobbied state legislatures for the passage of workmen's compensation acts. This program aimed, James Weinstein asserts, at endowing big business with a positive public image that would legitimize corporate control of American society.

The rhetoric of the financiers and industrialists who moved in the orbit of the Civic Federation proved equally enlightened in tone. "I think," observed George W. Perkins, J. P. Morgan's right-hand man, "where you have a large aggregate of money and of men in a corporation, you can get a public-service atmosphere that is much more advantageous to capital and labor than you can in smaller units of business." Added John D. Rockefeller, Jr.: "My appreciation of the conditions surrounding wage earners and my sympathy with every endeavor to better these conditions are as strong as those of any man." And John Hays Hammond, the world-famous mining engineer and entrepreneur noted: "I believe that employers of labor would do well to support labor organizations of that kind [AFL craft unions] to prevent the growth of organizations of the radical stripe."

Welfare capitalism and social harmony as practiced by the NCF and the industrialists who moved in its orbit proved chimerical. In practice, corporate welfare policies derived less from a concern for employees' betterment than from considerations of public image-making. In addition, the welfare measures introduced tended in reality to be available only to a small proportion of the total work force and were basically intended to avert unionization. If successful, welfare capitalism, by tying the worker to the corporation, transformed laborers into twentieth-century serfs, citizens in what a contemporary socialist labeled "Our Benevolent Feudalism."

If welfare capitalism was limited in its impact and perhaps undesirable in its effect, achieving social harmony was even more elusive. The same August Belmont who, as president of the NCF preached mediation, when confronted by a strike on his own transit lines in Brooklyn, practiced strikebreaking. And the steel companies and agricultural implement manufacturers directed by Perkins and Gary actively fought trade unionism among their workers. John D. Rockefeller, Jr., whose public comments revealed solicitude for the workingman, was also the owner of the Colorado Fuel and Iron Company, the concern associated with the single most violent and costly industrial conflict of the era: the Ludlow Massacre of 1914. In theory, employers preferred "responsible" to "radical" unions, nonsocialist to socialist unions; but, in practice, it was always another employer's union that seemed responsible and acceptable.

Smaller businessmen waged a war against organized labor that was at least consistent. More threatened by union power than their larger competitors, they had to fight labor more openly, if not more vigorously. As union membership rose steeply between 1897 and 1904, small businessmen organized themselves to fight back. The National Association of Manufacturers, originally established primarily to promote foreign trade, became in the twentieth century an institution geared to combat unions. Smaller employers also pooled their power in such antiunion organizations as the National Erectors' Association and the Citizens' Industrial Alliance, as well as in a variety of regional- and city-based antilabor associations. More prone to criticize unions openly and less willing to distinguish between "responsible" and "irresponsible" unions, these businessmen, too, sought to cultivate a positive public image. Their means was the ideology of individualism and liberty, rather than the practice of welfare and harmony. Their agency was the open-shop principle—the notion that each individual worker should be entirely free to join or *not* join a union and the corollary concept that no employer might discharge a nonunion member. In their avowed defense of individual liberty, such employers refused absolutely to negotiate with unions and to sign labor contracts. This, of course, made the worker's putative right to join a union (assuming his employer did not in fact discharge him for union membership, the usual course of action taken by open-shop bosses) meaningless, as unions denied the right to bargain with employers could offer no benefits to their members. It is also worth noting that most large industrialists shared the ideology of the open shop on the grounds of defending individual liberty. When ideology failed, the smaller businessmen, like the larger capitalists, used every means at their disposal—from strike-breakers, to private armed police, to spies and *agent provocateurs,* to militia, and court injunctions—to break strikes and unions. And like their big brothers, the smaller businesses succeeded more often than not in repulsing trade-union inroads.

THE AFL AND BUSINESS UNIONISM

In an environment hostile to labor organization but encouraging to effective organization and collective action, trade unions shed much of their nineteenth-century idealistic character. "Business unionism," as Philip Taft indicated, had historically always been a vital part of the craft-union tradition. But whereas in the past "business unionism" had been but one element in the union situation, it became during the Progressive period the dominant, sometimes sole, aspect of union behavior. Aping their corporate cousins, twentieth-century labor leaders sought to build more perfect organizations, ones in which the rank and file obediently followed the commands of bureaucratically inclined, well-paid officials. Indeed, in some of the more successful unions, such as the Carpenters and the Miners, the number of influential appointive positions rose substantially. In most stable labor organizations, officials elected to national and district positions consolidated their power by constructing a political machine built on a widening base of appointed subalterns who served at the pleasure of the elected officials. In some cases rebellious locals that challenged the emerging oligarchic tendencies in the labor movement had their charters suspended by the national union and found themselves mere wards of the international president. Where once union presidents were fortunate to serve multiple terms in office and maintained power largely through their oratorical abilities, they now could be defeated for reelection only in unusual circumstances and dominated their constituencies through administrative techniques.

The pattern of union bureaucratization was well illustrated by the AFL. In 1894 Gompers had been defeated for reelection. A year later he was restored to the presidency and held that position continuously until his death in 1924.

The practices and policies of the trade unions faithfully reflected their leaders' oligarchic tendencies. The educational and idealistic side of trade unionism lost its vigor as labor leaders concentrated on immediately achievable material objectives. The writings and speeches of Gompers and John Mitchell exemplified labor's changing self-image. Both labor leaders spiced thei. rhetoric with metaphors that likened the union to a responsible business institution, one providing optimal benefits for its stockholders (union members), dealing fairly with its adversaries (employers), and maintaining a due regard for the public interest. Union leaders pledged to hold labor contracts inviolate and to discipline members who broke signed agreements or provoked pointless disputes with conciliatory bosses. Inviolability of the labor contract meant in practice the death of the principle of solidarity, for unions that had signed contracts with employers refused to allow their members to walk off the job in sympathy with other workers who might have justifiable grievances against those same employers. So, just as industrialists sought to formalize and ritualize work processes through scientific management, labor leaders struggled to enmesh labor-management relations in a tight web of formal rules and procedures binding on both parties to the contract.

Even the nonbusiness side of the labor movement came to be influenced by the new conservatism and its oligarchic tendencies. Once the labor movement had swum vigorously against the tide;

now it began to float with the prevailing currents. In the 1880s and 1890s labor leaders had openly discussed alternatives to capitalism and had preached the principle of class conflict. After the turn of the century, however, officials such as Gompers and Mitchell castigated socialists as worse enemies of labor than capitalists and advocated the ideal of social harmony through membership in the NCF. As Gompers remarked to a congressional committee in 1913, "It is our duty to live our lives as workers in the society in which we live and not to work for the downfall or the destruction or the overthrow of that society, but for its fuller development and evolution."

Once partially immune to the national disease of racism, the labor movement became increasingly susceptible to the germ of white supremacy. Of course, Gompers and the AFL had consistently endorsed Asian exclusion. But by the early twentieth century black Americans and east and south European immigrants also came to be condemned on racialist grounds. Though the AFL and its historian, Philip Taft, might explain hostility to Negroes and immigrants as economic, not racialist—blacks broke strikes and immigrants undermined American wage levels and living standards—labor rhetoric told a different story. In 1904, the AFL printed in its official journal a condemnation of Negro strikebreakers in the Chicago stockyards which described them as "Hordes of ignorant blacks possessing but few of those attributes we have learned to revere and love, huge strapping fellows, ignorant and vicious, whose predominating trait was animalism." And criticism of newer immigrants tended to be couched in language stressing their alien, inferior character; labor leaders proved among the most adept at fathoming the "un-American."

The altered appearance of the labor movement could also be seen in the construction of new union headquarters and the changing clothes worn by union officials. As unions' income rose, they discontinued the customary practice of renting other people's buildings and instead built their own costly and elaborate headquarters. The AFL had heralded the new style in union headquarters in 1896 by moving its offices from

Indianapolis to Washington. And in Washington, where he appeared regularly on the social and political banquet circuit, Gompers dressed in a style more befitting a gentleman and business executive than a workingman or nineteenth-century labor leader. Simply by observing the shift in Gompers's dress, one might observe the American labor movement coming of age and catch a glimpse of the labor barons who would later sit across the bargaining table from America's business leaders. The AFL and its craft-union affiliates had come to be the comfortable home of a skilled, respectable, working-class elite.

At first, the more businesslike practices of the trade unions and their bureaucratic structures brought substantial gains. Between 1897 and 1904, for example, estimated union membership rose from 447,000 to 2,073,000. Not only did union membership soar as the economy boomed and unemployment declined, but unions also won significant improvements for their members. Some labor organizations even seemed able to bargain equally with employers' associations. A strike among bituminous coal miners in the Central Competitive Field (Western Pennsylvania, Ohio, Indiana, and Illinois) in 1897 was followed in 1898 by the Interstate Agreement between the United Mine Workers and the mine operators. This agreement stabilized labor-management relations in the Central Competitive Field, provided for union security, and improved working conditions (including the eight-hour day). The Interstate Agreement brought a quarter of a century of labor peace to bituminous mining in the North and great strength to the UMW, which grew from a membership of under 14,000 in 1897 to over 300,000 by 1914. In 1902 the Mine Workers won another major victory when, with the assistance of President Theodore Roosevelt, the union defeated the anthracite operators of northeastern Pennsylvania and opened the industry to trade unionism. Between 1898 and 1908, perhaps the most exclusive and tight-knit of all the AFL craft unions—the International Typographical Union—achieved the eight-hour day for its members in the printing trades. Another organization of highly skilled workers—the International Association of Machinists—used its growing membership and power to win the short-lived Murray Hill Agreement of 1900 from the National Metal Trades Association establishing an industry-wide nine-hour day. The Railroad Brotherhoods, which represented skilled employees on the nation's railroads, exercised their strength to obtain concessions from employers and also legislative protection from Congress. Moreover, many employers in the construction trades found themselves for a time at the mercy of quite avaricious and sometimes unscrupulous building trades unions in New York, Chicago, and San Francisco.

As labor power, especially among the skilled craft unionists flourished, employers reacted decisively. Businessmen and professionals in smaller industrial cities organized open-shop and antiboycott associations, which directly challenged the influence of trade unionism. Led by the National Association of Manufacturers and Citizens' Alliances locally, the employer counteroffensive pushed labor back with measurable success in the metal trades, where the Murray Hill Agreement was promptly terminated, and the building trades, where New York and Chicago contractors effectively reduced union control in the construction industry. Also between 1901 and 1909 United States Steel delivered the final blows to craft unionism in the steel industry, which, in effect, closed the mass-production industries to trade unionism until the 1930s. The depression of 1908–1909 that followed on the heels of the employers' antilabor offensive further decimated the ranks of trade unionism and, with one important exception, stymied trade-union growth until World War I.

The one exception to the retardation of union growth proved especially revealing of prevailing tendencies in American society and the labor movement. Between 1909 and 1913 almost 400,000 clothing workers joined the ranks of organized labor. At first glance, these workers appeared the unlikeliest union recruits—mostly minimally skilled women, Italian and East European Jewish immigrants. But in the nation's largest cities, especially New York and Chicago, where the clothing trades were centered, they organized, struck, and won. How and why? The answers we have are less than perfect. Most obviously the singular structure of the industry and the desire of many clothing manufacturers for a rationalization of their trade accounted for the acceptance of trade unionism. In an industry where a myriad of competing firms proved an insurmountable obstacle to business stabilization, an efficient union, by controlling the trade's major variable cost—labor—might provide the economic rationalization otherwise unavailable to employers.

Although economic factors opened the industry to unionization, traditional methods of labor organization proved unavailing. In industries where workers moved in and out of the trade continually or moved from firm to firm, where businesses failed regularly, slow and steady enrollment of union members seemed fruitless. The only alternative was labor's counterpart to the military blitzkrieg—a total industrywide strike. But strikes had proved notoriously chancy for American workers, especially for the weakly organized and the less skilled, the precise case of the garment workers. Here the assistance of middle-class reformers and political Progressives came to labor's assistance. When garment workers struck, especially in New York City, instead of meeting resistance by public authorities as well as employers, they found, at the least, municipal impartiality and sometimes direct, positive encouragement. For just as garment manufacturers desired business stability, which labor organizers promised to deliver through successful unionization of the trade's workers, reformers and public officials sought a happy paradise of law and order in industry constructed on the basis of negotations between responsible business and labor organizations supervised by neutral third-party arbitrators representing the public interest. Committed to impartial third-party intervention, the progressive reformers' approach to labor relations worked in an industry in which bosses were scarcely more powerful than their organized workers.

However, even in the garment industry, schemes to organize the workers succeeded only if the unions involved moved in bureaucratic and oligarchic directions. Employers tolerated unionism if it reduced competition in the industry by maintaining absolute uniformity of labor costs and practices; reformers and public officials applauded unionism if it produced industrial peace, meaning an end to strikes and lockouts; this proved no easy accomplishment for labor leaders who represented a singularly idealistic membership raised on an ideological diet of socialism, class conflict, and rank-and-file democracy. Throughout the Progressive period and later, officials in the needle trades unions desperately and regularly fought with an unruly and radical membership in an effort to maintain tighter national discipline over locals and to increase the effective authority of national officers. Also noteworthy is the fact that in an industry in which women workers predominated and in which they had proved such effective and militant strikers, no women held major national union office. Apparently, no union, regardless of its idealistic or radical origins, could escape either the bureaucratic imperative or male domination.

The garment workers' experience revealed why trade unionists declined to entrust labor's welfare to the mercy of nonworking-class reformers, no matter how public-spirited. Certainly the garment workers had benefited from middle-class assistance, but other labor disputes at the same time in different industries illuminated the naive beliefs that guided so many middle-class reformers. Indeed, the reformers often functioned in an idealized world divorced from the realities of economic power. In theory, their principles of industrial relations seemed grand. Management and labor should have equal rights, the one to keep employees out of unions, the other to recruit them; the company union and the independent union should compete freely; and impartial public mediators should guarantee that labor and capital respected each other's rights. But the real world was not that simple. Management, not union officials, controlled employment opportunities; bosses, not labor leaders, conferred wage increases and job promotions; businesses, not trade unions, possessed in most cases greater material resources. Ideals of equality and impartial public intervention proved meaningless when industrial disputants were of unequal strength, as some union leaders who relied on external assistance learned to their great dismay. Moreover, what reformers and public officials gave to labor they could later take back. Better for workers and their unions to rely entirely on their own resources and power, which meant first establishing and then sanctifying the principle of "voluntarism."

After 1900 "voluntarism" became the dominant doctrine among the unions associated with the AFL. The basic premise underlying the doctrine was the rudimentary notion that workers must defend their own interests in society. The premise itself derived from a combination of historical experience and common sense. Trade unionists had learned during the many brutal labor conflicts of the nineteenth century that the state was generally the enemy of workers. Federal and state troops had consistently broken strikes, and members of the judiciary had regularly enjoined workers from striking. Not only did the state serve as the enemy of labor, but politics within the trade unions divided workers and undermined their organizations. To look to government or to politics for salvation was to seek the useless. Success and security came only from power, and power in turn flowed from absolute union self-sufficiency. This meant that labor leaders used every means available to cultivate rank-and-file devotion to the union. All the workers' most vital needs—job security, unemployment relief, sickness and death benefits—must be met by the union, not the state. If government established compulsory welfare programs, reasoned labor leaders, the worker's loyalty to his union would be diluted with dire consequences for trade-union power. "Some men unconsciously and with best intentions," observed Gompers, "get to rivet chains on their wrists." Such logic led the AFL and its more powerful affiliates to oppose most government efforts to mandate maximum hours and minimum wages for adult men; to provide unemployment insurance; and to introduce social security legislation. In the hyperbole of Gompers, government efforts to control working conditions and the people's welfare "...is...the beginning of an era, and a long era, of industrial slavery."

In origin, then, the doctrine of voluntarism represented a logical response to a concrete historical situation—labor's oppression by employers and the state and the consequent need to build powerful, self-sufficient trade unions. But, as Michael P. Rogin has suggested, voluntarism became over time a formalized and abstract doctrine that bore little relation to the realities of American society. For one thing, most wage workers did not belong to unions. The vast majority desperately needed governmental action to improve their conditions and secure their welfare. Although AFL spokesmen emphasized publicly that the labor movement served the entire working class, their actions belied their rhetoric. Voluntarism, Rogin concludes, rather than defending the mass of workers against a hostile state, protected strong craft unions and oligarchic labor leaders from necessary public control and rank-and-file pressures for change. As an abstract doctrine, voluntarism became the first line of defense for private labor governments devoted to the advancement of narrow economic interest groups.

But just as the principle of voluntarism carried to reductionist conclusions rendered a disservice to the mass of American workers, an equally abstract analysis of the doctrine obfuscates a substantial element of AFL and trade-union activities in the Progressive period. The ideal model of voluntarism implied that trade unionists steered clear of party politics and never became enmeshed in the gears of government. That ideal, however, conflicted with two inescapable realities: 1) politics and government inevitably impinged on trade-union security; 2) trade-union members were not solely economic men; they were also citizens in a larger social and political community. These two factors increasingly compelled labor leaders to enter politics themselves.

Two considerations motivated the AFL's political activities. On the one hand, a series of crippling antilabor judicial decisions impelled trade unionists to act politically in order to secure themselves against court injunctions. On the other hand, an avalanche of requests by state federations of labor and city centrals for independent political action motivated Gompers and his associates to go political, lest the AFL lose control of its local labor bodies or see working-class voters veer more sharply in a socialist direction. The first factor was probably the more important, as the judicial threat to union security seemed dire and immediate. Also, it was comparable to the situation in England where, as a result of two judicial decisions harmful to organized labor among other factors, British workers had become aggressively political and founded what would become the British Labour Party. The AFL was not unmindful of the British experience; an editorial in its official journal observed: "If the British workmen, with their limited franchise, accomplished so much by their united action, what may we in the United States not do with universal suffrage?"

To see what labor in the United States might do politically, the AFL executive council in 1906 adopted Labor's Bill of Grievances, a list of the AFL's most desired legislative goals, which it presented to President Roosevelt and Republican congressional leaders for action. Dissatisfied with the Republican response, the executive council next organized a Labor Representation Committee, led by Gompers, which promised to campaign for candidates friendly to labor and in favor of the AFL's political program. As the 1908 presidential campaign approached, the AFL intensified its political activities. It scheduled a special political protest conference in Washington, and the Labor Representation Committee drew up a program for presentation to the major party nominating conventions. Rebuffed by the Republicans but wooed by the Democrats, in 1908 Gompers and the AFL entered into an informal political entente with the Democratic party. Four years later that entente grew firmer and more open during Woodrow Wilson's campaign for the presidency. When Wilson actually delivered political rewards to his labor advocates, the national alliance between the AFL and the Democrats was consummated. In 1916 the AFL executive council members and most trade-union leaders, with an exception or two, made no effort to hide their support of the Wilson Democrats. During World War I, as we shall see in the next chapter, the AFL-Democratic alliance was made firmer, as trade-union officials were drawn directly into the government.

If organized labor, as represented by the AFL, became more active in national politics, the real nature of working-class politics revealed itself most clearly at the state and local levels. State and municipal regulations still had more effect on most trade unions than federal labor laws. Locally, too, workers, whether organized or not, belonged to social communities that influenced their political beliefs and responses. Working-class politics at the local level also illustrated most starkly the factors curbing labor's political power. Unfortunately, however, with the exception of New York City and California, we have little substantial information about working-class political behavior. A few tentative observations can be offered. Working-class political unity was exceptional, if indeed it ever occurred. The major lines dividing workers seem to be ethnic and religious, with northern American-born Protestant and north European Protestant workers leaning toward Republicanism; Irish Catholic workers providing the electoral base for many a city Democratic machine; Jewish immigrants evincing a notable political independence and in some cases a tendency toward socialism; and other east and south European immigrants, either leaning toward Republicanism or lacking the franchise in significant numbers. Organized workers, at least in so far as the public expressions of their leaders indicated, appeared politically more independent than the unorganized, who tended to be more loyal toward bosses and local machines. But it should be observed that in most cities the building and printing trades unions were usually in open alliance with the dominant local machine—Republican in Philadelphia, Democratic in New York and Boston. This was a simple case of self-interest, for building inspectors and city building codes could be used to strengthen trade-union power, while the extent of public printing made it wise to keep the business in union shops. Much more research and analysis remains to be done, however, before we can draw firmer conclusions about working-class political behavior in Progressive America.

Whether operating through the preferred means of economic power or through politics, the AFL and its affiliated unions seemed to serve their members well. Representing those with skill and bargaining power, trade unions succeeded in winning material gains by ensuring that their reach seldom exceeded their grasp. Whether it would have been wiser for the trade unions to have risked more for larger objectives is a difficult question. Suffice it to say that in an environment notably hostile to labor organization, the AFL and the craft unions survived, and, on their own limited terms, even thrived. But in 1914, as Engels had observed in 1893, the trade unions remained a sanctuary for an aristocracy of American labor, quite willing to neglect the mass of less fortunate workers who lacked the means or ability to form unions of their own.

RADICAL UNIONISM AND SOCIALISM

Having preempted the center and right wings of the labor spectrum, the AFL left room for opposition and criticism solely on the left. Hence, within the labor movement and from outside, hostility toward the AFL originated among radicals with a socialist or syndicalist tendency. Yet these radicals were themselves divided in their attitudes and reactions to the trade unions. Some leftists sought to destroy the "reactionary" AFL; others desired mutual coexistence; and still others preferred to function within the trade unions and eventually convert them to radicalism. For a time during the Progressive years, when labor radicals reached their apogee in America, they appeared to threaten the AFL's tenuous hegemony over the nation's working class.

How great the radical threat to the trade unions and American society actually was remains debatable. But each time socialists won a local political victory or workers walked off their jobs under radical leadership, major party politicians, the newspapers, and academic commentators warned citizens of the rising socialist or syndicalist tide. More perceptive observers of the American scene, rather than simply condemning or ridiculing the radicals, tried to understand their motives and goals. One sympathetic academician, Louis Levine, in an essay written in 1913, put his finger squarely on the source of the American radical movement. "The forces which drove American toilers to blaze new paths, to forge new weapons and to reinterpret the meaning of life in new terms were," Levine wrote, "the struggles and compromises, the adversities and successes, the exultation and despair born of conditions of life in America."

The reasons for left-wing opposition to the AFL are almost too obvious to mention. Any radical could see that the trade unions, as then constituted, lacked the desire or ability to organize the great mass of American workers and, moreover, were isolated from the dominant sectors of the national economy—such mass-production industries as steel, meat-packing, autos, rubber, and electrical goods. In addition, the advanced technology of modern large-scale industry rendered the craft unionism and exclusive jurisdiction of most AFL affiliates ineffective. The history of unsuccessful efforts to organize the basic industries and of failed strikes demonstrated the AFL's inability to serve the semiskilled workers who in the more technologically advanced sectors of the economy formed an undifferentiated mass. In other words, the craft unions may have been an eminently successful response to mid-nineteenth-century conditions, and they may have continued to work well for laborers in the more traditional, skilled trades, but for that very reason, they had less to offer the millions of semiskilled machine operators in basic industry.

The split between the AFL and the political left became more pronounced after the turn of the century. Before the late 1890s, the AFL and radicals had maintained amicable relations, perhaps because both groups were so weak that they desperately needed each other's support. But as the AFL grew more stable and radicals more ambitious, friction developed. Daniel DeLeon's frontal attack on the trade unions in the 1890s had already driven a wedge between the AFL and the socialists. Gompers and his lieutenants would neither forgive nor forget DeLeon's sectarian tactics, a fact which thereafter embittered trade-union relations with the vast majority of anti-DeLeon American socialists. In addition, the trade unions' evolving accommodation with capitalism, as strikingly revealed in the National Civic Federation, occurred just as American socialism entered its golden age, from 1900 to 1917. With the two factions of the working-class movement going in opposite directions, a crash seemed imminent.

Yet it is much too easy to exaggerate the division between trade unionists and socialists. One must remember that Samuel Gompers and John Mitchell were not the only trade-union leaders in America; nor did they necessarily reflect the sentiments of most workers. Despite Gompers's bitter attacks on the socialists, socialism gained substantial financial and organizational support from several trade unions and most of its votes came from the working class. Indeed, in places where the Socialist Party of America proved most successful—Milwaukee, the Massachusetts shoe towns, New York City, Bridgeport, Connecticut, and Butte, Montana, among others—its links to the trade unions and to the working class were tightest. Socialism's appeal to the working class transcended regional, craft, and ethnic lines. Six national unions which endorsed socialism—the United Mine Workers, the Boot and Shoe Workers, the International Association of Machinists, the United Brewery Workers, the Western Federation of Miners, and the Ladies' Garment Workers—represented American-born and foreign-born workers, east European and north European immigrants, Catholics, Jews, and Protestants, craftsmen and industrial workers, urban and rural employees, and the northeastern, southern, and western regions of the nation.

Because such unions and also many unorganized workers favored socialism, the Socialist party's national vote rose appreciably between 1900 and 1912. More significant than increases in the party's presidential vote were electoral victories, which in many parts of the country placed municipal administrations in socialist hands, returned numerous socialists to state legislatures, and elected Victor Berger of Milwaukee and Meyer London of New York to Congress. The socialist vote, as many contemporary and later observers were to notice, seemed to peak in the state and local elections of 1911 and thereafter to diminish. But it must be borne in mind that the areas in which the socialist vote declined most notably after 1911-1912—rural Western and

Southern states (Massachusetts was the exception that proved the rule)—were perhaps the least decisive for the future of American socialism. In the urban, industrial, and immigrant working-class areas of the nation, the socialist vote did not peak in 1912, and would not do so until the World War I years. At no time before the end of the war, then, could one say firmly that American socialism was dead, or that the working class had rejected left-wing alternatives.

Before proceeding further it should be stressed that this discussion of socialism is restricted to those factions and individuals clustered around the Socialist Party of America, which was formed in 1901. The original party of the American left—the Socialist Labor Party—had become by then a narrow sect of true believers whose doctrines were expounded *ex cathedra* by the dogmatic Daniel DeLeon. DeLeon and his few followers were purists and perfectionists, who scorned reform, ridiculed the trade unions and their leaders as the labor lieutenants of capitalism, and preached true revolution. Paradoxically, the SLP's insignificance allowed it to retain its revolutionary purity. Never blessed with a mass following, never an electoral winner, never having to confront the actual uses of power, the SLP and its members could maintain their doctrinal perfectionism in an imperfect world.

Everything the SLP was not, the Socialist Party of America was. Unlike Daniel Bell's socialists, who were religious sectarians *in* an imperfect world but not *of it*, and who were also moral perfectionists unable to make the political compromises essential to an imperfect world, the prewar socialists in fact were realists and reformers who built a third party comparable in structure to the two major political parties. Like the Republicans and Democrats, the Socialists had their regional and ideological differences, which they fought out within party councils. Like the Republicans and Democrats, Socialists could ordinarily harmonize their internal differences at election time. But unlike Republicans and Democrats, Socialists usually lacked the glue of patronage; they had to maintain their coalition on the basis of shared values, not the spoils of office. What held Socialists together was a transcendent belief in a better and more moral cooperative society, which could be built through the efforts of a united, class-conscious working class. Socialists, however, were divided about how to attain their new society and how to radicalize the workers.

The dominant wing of American socialism, influenced by Victor Berger and Morris Hillquit, cultivated trade-union support. Although Eugene Debs, the most prominent American left-winger and the party's presidential candidate on five separate occasions, openly criticized the AFL and occasionally joined with declared enemies of trade unionism, Berger and Hillquit formulated a party trade-union policy that proclaimed: "The Socialist Party is absolutely committed to a policy of friendship to organized labor, and unequivocally recognizes the A. F. of L. of today as the main representative of organized labor." In practice this meant that most socialists sought to influence the AFL's affiliates toward industrial unionism with a political aspect.

Despite their apocalyptic rhetoric, most American socialists tended to be piecemeal reformers. The political party and the trade union acted as the twin pillars of their ultimate revolution. Party politics would bring immediate legislative reforms and then ultimate control of the state, which would nationalize the basic means of production and distribution. Trade unions would win immediate concessions from employers, educate their members regarding political action, and train workers to administer the cooperative commonwealth's publicly owned industries. Within this general framework of attempted accommodation with the trade unions and reformism, socialism constantly changed direction, as it confronted such divisive issues as immigration, racism, and war and peace. "The socialist movement," observed Hillquit, "has changed its practical methods somewhat. It always does. It learns from experience."

This shifting, moderate, and "pragmatic" socialist movement, which sank deep roots in the trade unions and among the working class between 1900 and 1917, has left scarcely a trace on latter-day American society. Why? Daniel Bell's suggestion that socialism declined because of its sectarian, otherworldly, perfectionist, utopian nature seems wrong. The customary explanation for the failure of socialism contends that while indigenous American conditions generated a left-wing political movement, they also doomed it. Lacking a feudal tradition, American society, in the conventional view, failed to provide the firm class structure which motivated workers in the face of adversity to remain socialist. In a society without tight class lines, in which wages were relatively high, and where social mobility existed, socialism's attraction to workers proved impermanent. Moreover, the major parties consistently preempted socialism's reform appeal; this was especially true in the aftermath of Wilson's election in 1912, when the Democratic party successfully wooed several previously socialist-inclined trade unions and undermined socialism's appeal in such states as Massachusetts and Illinois. In short, a liberal society, having produced "people of plenty," offers nothing but stony soil for socialist seeds. To this explanation may be added the basically Leninist notion that political socialism and trade unionism are incompatible. A major theme of many labor histories, for example, is the idea that as unions mature and gain tangible benefits for their members, the appeal of socialism inevitably diminishes; in fact, John Laslett has argued that a trade union commitment to socialist politics renders its bread-and-butter activities ineffective. One is thus left with the following paradox: socialists, almost without exception, believed that organized workers were easier to radicalize than the unorganized and that they made better socialists; Laslett, however, tells us that the more successful was trade-union organization, the fewer trade unionists found socialism appealing.

Other explanations for the failure of socialism in the world's leading capitalist nation have also been propounded. Rather than ascribing socialism's limited appeal to the absence of feudalism, American prosperity, the durability of the two-party system, or the foolish policies of leftists, some scholars such as James Weinstein and James Green cite state repression during World War I and communist sectarianism afterward as primary causes for the collapse of the SPA. That interpretation, however, fails to explain why socialists in other belligerent industrial nations, who also endured wartime repression and then suffered communist opposition, grew stronger afterwards. Why did socialism remain a vital force in French, German, British and Scandinavian society? What made the American situation different?

The answer to American exceptionalism in this case requires a more careful and precise comparison between structures and events in the United States and those occurring at the same time in other advanced industrial countries. Even without such a detailed comparison, it appears that the following factors were decisive in the American case: 1) the achievement of universal manhood suffrage prior to the emergence of political socialism; 2) the peculiarities of American national political culture; 3) the Democratic Party's successful courtship of the trade unions between 1908 and 1918; 4) the ethno-religious and racial lines which fractured the working class politically as well as culturally; and 5) the open rift between the leadership of the dominant labor federation (AFL) and the socialists, which existed to the same intensity in no other country.

Political socialists, however, were not alone in challenging the hegemony of the trade unions and in offering American workers an alternative to capitalism. At the same time that socialism reached its American zenith, the most famous, feckless, and adventurous labor radicals in United States history arrived on the scene. In June 1905 a small band of labor radicals, left-wing socialist from both the SLP and the SPA, and dissatisfied craft unionists gathered in convention in Chicago to form the Industrial Workers of the World, better known to history as the Wobblies. At this convention, which William D. "Big Bill" Haywood declared the "Continental Congress of the American working class," delegates voted to establish a national labor organization in competition with the AFL, one which would organize workers along industrial, not craft, lines and which would wage unrelenting class war against the capitalists until the existing system of society and government was overthrown. Dedicated to the interment of capitalism in America, the Wobblies appealed to those workers neglected by the trade unions and exploited by society. As Eugene Debs, a convention delegate and early advocate of the IWW put it: "The choice is between the A.F. of L. and capitalism on one side and the industrial workers and socialism on the other."

Born in a burst of enthusiasm and noble purpose, the IWW during its first years was wracked by internal discord and almost destroyed by reckless tactics. SLP'ers and SPA members, bitter enemies of long standing, continued to fight each other within the IWW. Their own political fortunes seemed more important than organization of the unorganized. Trade unionists at times proved equally disruptive to the new radical organization. They could not make up their minds whether to create new unions for workers excluded from the AFL or whether to capture the existing trade unions. As a result, Wobblies wasted too much of their limited energy and scarce funds in warring with AFL affiliates, which were not about to submit to upstart radicals. To compound matters, the political socialists and trade unionists in the IWW were constantly at each other's throats. One by one, prominent Socialist Party adherents broke away from the IWW when it seemed unable to organize industrial workers, their divorce from the Wobblies culminating with Debs's quiet departure in 1907. That same year, the Western Federation of Miners, the largest single trade-union affiliate of the IWW, walked out. And a year later, the small remnant that then claimed title to the IWW purged Daniel DeLeon and his SLP followers from the organization. All that remained in 1908 of the radical coalition founded in 1905 was a tiny band of labor radicals united in their rejection of business unionism, suspicious of all political parties, socialist included, and committed primarily to direct action by workers at the point of production. What remained of the original IWW had no mass following, not enough money to publish a paper or to pay regular organizers, and apparently no future.

Yet over the next decade this small band of labor radicals would vex employers, governors, congressmen, cabinet members, and American presidents. By World War I some Americans considered the Wobblies as great a threat to national security as German imperialists and Russian Bolsheviks. Neither before nor since has any group of labor radicals been as feared as the Wobblies, nor as vindictively repressed.

Why the Wobblies evoked such fear remains a troublesome question. All students of the IWW agree that the organization never gained a mass membership, even at its peak in 1917; that while Wobblies proved adept at organizing and administering spontaneous working-class eruptions, they were less successful in building stable organizations; and, finally, that Wobblies were torn between striving for total revolution and gaining immediate reforms. Perhaps fear of the Wobblies derived from what they said and to whom they appealed, not what they actually did. Their speeches and writings were filled with threatening similes and dark metaphors in which figurative violence appeared repeatedly. And their primary audience consisted of recent immigrants, black Americans, and restless migratories and itinerants of every sort—all in all, a volatile, even explosive, mixture. If the IWW failed to organize a mass membership at any single point in time, over the course of its halcyon days from 1909 to 1918, some two to three million workers passed through its ranks and millions more were subject to its influence. Its cadres also seemed ubiquitous, as Wobblies cropped up at all of the great industrial battles of the period—McKees Rocks, Pennsylvania in 1909; Lawrence, Massachusetts in 1912; Paterson, New Jersey, and Akron, Ohio in 1913; Wheatland, California in 1915; the Mesabi Range and Everett, Washington in 1916; and the forests and copper mines of Montana, Arizona, Idaho, Oregon and Washington State in 1917-1918. Wherever the Wobblies went to fight for free speech or struggle for better working conditions, tumult and violence followed. Indeed, the IWW proved the best single barometer of the violence hidden behind the facade of an age of reform.

Contemporaries could not agree about the aims and ideology of the IWW, and neither can subsequent generations of scholars despite a recent spate of publications about the IWW. Many scholars, after a few passing overtures to the Wobblies' romantic spirit and sense of daring, have followed the Perlman-Taft tradition of deprecating the IWW as an association of gunslinging frontiersmen representative of a passing way of life, as an organization more famous for its songs than its accomplishments, for its oratory rather than its organizing, and hence ultimately an organization, which because it offered at best an oversimplified, antipolitical Marxism, withered on the political vine without leaving many tangible fruits.

Although disputes still occur among historians concerning whether the Wobblies were reformers or revolutionaries, political activists or apolitical organizers of the working class, industrial unionists or syndicalists, it now seems clear that the IWW represented a valid response to an emerging way of life, not a reaction to a lost past. It was also more often the victim rather than the perpetrator of violence. On the other hand, Wobblies were reformers in the American grain, industrial unionists in a tradition that runs from the Knights of Labor to the CIO, and a vital part of the socialist coalition until expelled by the party in 1913. On the other hand, however, Wobblies were never ones to disguise their revolutionary principles, nor to dismiss their many breaches of American political and cultural traditions.

Overall, it seems a mistake to draw too sharp a dichotomy between reform and revolution. The two goals may be mutually exclusive but that remains to be proved. Because individual Wobblies in numerous circumstances chose to seek immediate gains, or to accept them when offered, does not make those Wobblies any less revolutionary. The same Wobbly who struck for higher wages, shorter hours, or better food would not sign a binding contract with his boss that might tie labor's hands in the event of changed conditions. He desired to be free to fight the class war at any time in any way he chose. As Elizabeth Gurley Flynn reminded fellow IWW members in the aftermath of defeat in Paterson, strikes are waged more to instill class consciousness and revolutionary spirit in the working class than to win a few pennies more an hour. Better to lose a strike in which workers learned that employers were the enemy, she observed, than to return to work with better conditions and a diluted consciousness of class. Certainly the Wobblies preached industrial unionism in response to what they considered the craft basis of the AFL. But if that was the sole basis of their conflict with the AFL, they were naive and mistaken radicals, for the AFL showed that its structure could encompass industrial unions by inclusion of the United Mine Workers, the Brewery Workers, and the Ladies' Garment Workers.

What the Wobblies symbolized, then, was more than industrial unionism. They stood for a conception of society in which workers, when fully organized and class conscious, could by direct action at the point of production seize the nation's industries and administer them by and for the working class without political parties and the state as intermediaries. If that is a rough definition of syndicalism, and I think it is, then the Wobblies were indeed syndicalists. And because they were syndicalists, they followed a consistent policy of dissociation from political parties and political action, which, to be sure, did not preclude individual Wobblies from voting for the party most sympathetic to labor. They turned against political action because, as syndicalists, they believed that socialist parties everywhere had become too opportunistic in their search for votes. Instead of intensifying working-class consciousness and militancy, Socialist politicians counseled moderation and class collaboration in order to win respectability and still more votes. Wobblies also had practical reasons for their apolitical approach; the workers whom they organized most successfully and appealed to most often lacked the franchise. American-born migratories, the IWW majority in the West and South, moved too often to establish voting residences; new immigrants were aliens, often confused by complicated electoral procedure, and also spatially mobile; and women, child workers, and nonwhites were simply disfranchised. Of what use was politics to those exploited groups? Finally, it seems to me to be of more than passing interest that in the same year that the IWW was founded, Italian and French national labor bodies adopted syndicalist positions, and that in a few years syndicalist sentiments would spread to Great Britain and its overseas dominions. It might be wiser to comprehend the IWW experience, not in terms of unique American conditions, but as part of the general process of capitalist growth in the industrial world where all countries had their own singular cultures and conditions but where all workers, regardless of nationality, tasted the fruits, bitter and sweet, of industrial capitalism.

Though the Wobblies, like the Socialists, failed to revolutionize American society, they, too, raised serious questions about working-class organization, the sufficiency of political democracy in a society in which economic power was so unevenly distributed, and the nature and basis of corporate power. At a time when civil liberties were respected more in the breach than in practice, Wobblies challenged local authorities through campaigns of civil disobedience. At a time when nonwhite Americans and new immigrants formed an oppressed and submerged proletariat within an increasingly prosperous America, Wobblies attempted to stir them from lethargy and lift them from the mudsill of society. Wobblies taught the outcasts and orphans of society that power is gained through organization, and that only power moves men and societies. The poor, Wobblies preached, must organize to achieve the power which alone could improve their condition. If their ideas stimulated the poor to help themselves, their actions revealed the gap between American ideals of equality and brotherhood and their practice, the distance between notions of a society based on law, not men, and one in which those with social and economic power abused or ignored the law in order to oppress the weak.

AGE OF INDUSTRIAL VIOLENCE

Before leaving the Progressive period behind to see what happened to American workers during World War I, several final observations must be made. We think, and so far the pages of this book have not done enough to dispel that image, of the late nineteenth century as a time of labor turbulence, sharp class conflict, and untold violence, while the Progressive period glows bright with fires of reform, progress, and social harmony. But that only goes to show what fine mythmakers we historians are. Graham Adams, Jr., may not have been far off the mark when he entitled a book on labor relations in the Progressive era *Age of*

Industrial Violence (1966). What Adams does, and quite effectively at that, is to portray the ugly social sores still festering in an age of reform.

No simple list or recitation of the bitter industrial battles waged in the early twentieth century can do full justice to the human drama and suffering involved, but such a list can remind the student of the continuity of industrial violence in American history. From 1903 to 1905 members of the Western Federation of Miners and mine owners and smelter operators in Colorado waged a literal war, which featured private armies of gunmen, shooting, and dynamiting. When the state intervened, owing to a rising toll of lives and property damage, militia commanders suspended legal due process, openly intimidated judges, cooperated with private vigilante groups in persecuting union members and sympathizers, instituted martial law, and deported several score union members from Colorado without trial or formal hearing. Ten years later (1914) coal miners in the same state went out on strike only to face company-hired gunmen-criminals deputized as law officers by county sheriffs—and the state militia that, in the infamous Ludlow Massacre, raked a tent camp of strikers' families with savage gunfire. Apparently unable to discriminate between men, women, or children, nor content to shoot at women and children, the Colorado militia put the strikers' camp to the torch, an incendiary act which cost the lives of a miner's entire family. In between those two struggles in Colorado, violent industrial conflicts rocked the coal fields of West Virginia, railroad towns in Illinois, Iowa, Mississippi, and Louisiana, the forests of the Pacific Northwest, the iron mining region of northern Minnesota, and the old mill towns of the Northeast. These, remember, were the years of McKees Rocks, Lawrence, Paterson, and countless other less famous but equally costly struggles.

If the early twentieth century seems a less chaotic era in industrial relations than the preceding quarter of a century, that is more a construct of historical social science than a measure of reality. Because the Progressive era was clearly a more bureaucratized, rationalized, and administratively orderly time than the Gilded Age, its labor relations do in retrospect appear less chaotic and violent. Such images of stability were also fostered by the fact that fewer strikes were spontaneous and more were union-sponsored and administered. Still, strikes occurred three times as often in the early twentieth century, witnessed their fair share of violence, and, because there were more of them involving substantially larger numbers of workers, caused a higher toll of human casualties. To some contemporaries labor-capital conflict seemed so endemic and destabilizing that they demanded a federal investigation of industrial relations. Presidents Taft and Wilson deferred to those demands by establishing the U.S. Commission on Industrial Relations (1912–1915), which made one of the most thorough investigations ever undertaken on the subject.

The formation of the federal commission was precipitated by an event in which labor was the perpetrator, not the victim. In 1911 members of the Iron and Structural Workers' Union dynamited the Los Angeles *Times* building because the paper's owner-publisher, Harrison Gray Otis, was a leader of the open-shop movement in southern California. This explosion, which took the lives of twenty people, was the culmination of a series of dynamitings intended to intimidate antiunion employers. From the Molly Maguires of the 1870s to a series of explosions which blasted Butte, Montana in 1914, then, American workers and employers wrote a tragic history compounded in equal parts of despair and violence.

But as the Progressive era drew to an end, workers could look back upon a decade and a half of substantial welfare reforms, and organized labor could reflect upon its new status as a vital member of the political coalition ruling the nation in Washington. Woodrow Wilson's warm embrace of Gompers and the AFL was only a foreshadowing of the ties that would bind organized labor ever closer to national government during World War I. Developments barely visible in the Progressive period would come to full flower during the war years.

This labor movement of ours is an American labor movement, not a Hebrew labor movement or a heathen labor movement.

SAMUEL GOMPERS

The world is in the midst of a new social era—the establishment of the principles of social democracy...

SIDNEY HILLMAN

FOUR

Workers and World War, 1914–1920

War inspires man as well as degrades him; it builds new social structures as well as destroys established ones; it provides innumerable and previously unimaginable opportunities for reform as well as singular occasions for repression; it is an event, on the one hand, to be viewed with foreboding and anxiety, and, on the other hand, to be greeted with joy and relief. Of no conflict was this truer than World War I, which brought to a violent close nearly a full century of relative peace among the world's leading industrial and military powers.

As war raged on European battlefields from 1914 into early 1917, Americans, too, felt its impact. Paradoxically, many citizens who had been in the vanguard of pacifist and antiwar movements in the pre-1914 years became strong advocates of American intervention and total defeat of Imperial Germany. They saw war as a necessity not just to thwart German autocracy in order to make the "world safe for democracy"; it was also perceived as an opportunity to achieve at home the social reforms which had eluded peacetime America. War, perhaps, would provide the occasion for the implementation of a general welfare state. For reformers who thought in such terms, World War I, as James Weinstein has observed, "was fulfillment."

War also brought to a climax developments within the American working class and its labor movement that had been building for half a century. Suddenly the social and economic environment favored, rather than thwarted, trade unionism. Working-class militancy exploded with singular intensity during the war years. An opportunity now existed for workers to build organizations as effective and powerful as national business corporations. American involvement in the war also appeared to intensify working-class consciousness, and this war-induced class consciousness affected relations between employees and employers, laborers and government, workers and their unions. Finally, war brought to fruition organized labor's long effort to influence the national government directly and to win federal sanction for its goals. Wartime interaction between AFL officials and the federal government led President Wilson to admit "loyal" labor leaders to the inner ranks of the national political establishment. War for workers and labor leaders could also be fulfillment.

WAR AND WORKERS

The most immediate impact of the war on workers was economic—and harmful. In the early summer of 1914, the United States was entering a deep depression, one that would fit quite well into a recurrent historical pattern of economic breakdowns every twenty years (1857, 1873, 1893, and 1913). So severe did the impending economic breakdown seem likely to become that, for example, in New York City, the mayor created a special municipal committee on unemployment to cope with the city's jobless, a group fast approaching 30 percent of the labor force. However extreme New York may have been as an example of unemployment and economic collapse, joblessness was on the rise everywhere in the nation in 1914, a situation aggravated by the European war's shattering impact on international trading networks.

War, however, quickly proved a blessing in disguise to America's workers, particularly as their nation chose to remain neutral. For several decades prior to 1914 organized labor had lobbied assiduously, but ineffectively, to restrict immigration to America. Using a combination of racialist and economic arguments, though stressing the latter, the AFL's leaders had sought to put a literacy test requirement for immigrants into law—but to no avail. War, of course, accomplished what political lobbying failed to achieve. After August 1914 there was no legal escape from the belligerent European nations for millions of prospective emigrants—the world war ended three and a half decades of mass immigration to America. At the same time that war effectively reduced the size of the American labor market, it stimulated the demand for workers as a result of rising European orders for American goods. For two years, from mid-1915 to April 1917, American workers and businessmen prospered on European orders.

As unemployment fell in 1915 and 1916, while prices surged up, workers became more militant. This was especially true among organized workers who began to use the strike weapon as never before. Between 1915 and 1916 the number of reported strikes more than doubled, and the latter year recorded more industrial disputes than any previous time in the United States history—3789 as compared to 1589 in 1915. The strike fever raged with singular intensity in the munitions and armaments industry—particularly in strike-torn Bridgeport, Connecticut—

in which machinists and metal workers walked out to win higher wages and the eight-hour day. The contagion could not be checked. In 1915 and 1916, New Jersey oil refinery hands struck; clothing workers in New York walked off the job; steel workers in Youngstown stopped work; IWW-led iron miners on Minnesota's Mesabi Range marched in picket lines; and even migratory grain harvesters on the Great Plains threatened job action against their farmer employers.

Rank-and-file militancy peaked in New York City where a 1916 strike by transit workers threatened to turn into a city-wide general strike. In September 1916 the official representatives of the New York City and state labor movement recommended "a sympathetic strike of all organized wage earners in their jurisdiction in support of the contention of the ... railway men for the right to organize." Though Gompers equivocated in endorsing a full-scale general strike, he, too, counseled concerted action. In their newspapers New Yorkers read that between 200,000 and 500,000 strikers were about to cut the arteries of commerce and life. Stories detailed the crisis to be faced by the city the day the wheels of industry ground to a halt. The ugly visage of social revolution seemed to be rearing its head at the gateway to the American nation. In the event, however, the fears proved unwarranted. Union leaders proved more cautious and perhaps more prudent than their militant followers. Local, state, and national AFL officials, especially those associated with the building trades unions, tightened the reins on local unions and discouraged sympathy strikes. When the threatened general strike failed to materialize and the transit workers lost their struggle for union recognition, a socialist union observed: "It takes more than vulgar bluff to subdue the thugs of corporate capital." The New York City experience of 1916 illustrated the awakened militancy among workers as well as the persistence of managerial power and AFL caution.

Once more in 1916 as trade unions moved from the defensive to the offensive, union membership rose appreciably, especially among labor organizations active in war-related industries. The higher prices soared and the tighter the labor market grew the more militant and effective became organized workers and their trade unions.

But the economic plight of the unorganized who lacked unions to protect them against wage inflation must not be exaggerated. Prices may indeed have outrun wages, triggering food riots in many of the nation's largest cities in early 1917. Although thousands of immigrant wives took to the streets upturning neighborhood food pushcarts, putting overpriced produce to the torch, and threatening small grocers and butchers, for most workers inflation with a job was preferable to deflation without work. Moreover, we cannot be certain that income rose less rapidly than the cost of living. Indeed, there could be no dispute that millions of workers were now employed, and with greater job security than ever.

America's entry into the war in April 1917 provided further economic benefits for the nation's worker. The United States had to confront the same labor problem as the other belligerents had earlier faced. With their supply of immigrant workers cut off, American employers watched anxiously as first voluntary enlistments and then national conscription reduced their existing labor force. At a time when full production was vital to the war effort, skilled workers and millions of laborers were being conscripted. Hence civilian workers labored longer hours for increased income, and new sources of labor were tapped bringing millions of hitherto unemployed or unemployable workers steady jobs in industry.

Three sources provided employers with the bulk of their new labor force. Southern black migration to the North, which had been a small but steady stream from the end of Reconstruction to 1914, reached new proportions after American entry into the war. Some 200,000 to 300,000 southern blacks migrated to the regions associated with heavy industries and the production of primary metal products—Pittsburgh-Youngstown, Cleveland-Akron, Chicago-Gary, St. Louis-East St. Louis. For a half-century outdistanced in the job market by preferred white European immigrants, black native-born Americans were suddenly wanted, if not preferred. The same could be said of another dark-skinned group—Americans of Mexican origin and Mexicans by birth, residence, and citizenship. They, too, headed toward the centers of heavy industry. These two nonwhite groups would become a decisive factor in the mass strikes for union recognition which affected the meatpacking and steel industries in 1918 and 1919. Women were the third source of new workers, including many American-born females who had previously been reluctant to enter industrial work.

While new recruits to the labor force filled out the ranks of the unskilled and semiskilled, east and south European immigrants who once composed the mudsill of the industrial labor force improved their skills and jobs, as they earned positions once reserved for American-born or north European immigrant workers. In other words, hitherto socially and economically marginal individuals and groups, people whose main function had been to form a reserve labor army, now became citizen-workers, essential parts of the national war machine.

Wartime economic and demographic changes intensified the working-class and union militancy which had first erupted in 1915 and 1916. Between April 6, 1917 (when Congress declared war) and October 6, 1917, 3000 strikes occurred, including 407 in the vital mining industries. A total of over 4400 strikes were reported in 1917, and in that year and also in 1918, for the first time in American history over one million workers annually walked off the job. Between September 1917 and April 1918 citywide strikes in Springfield, Illinois, Kansas City, Missouri, Waco, Texas, and Billings, Montana disconcerted federal officials. No sector of the economy escaped industrial conflict. Telephone operators, packinghouse workers, longshoremen, loggers, copper miners, and grain harvesters all struck vital war industries. Even the most conservative unions were not above using the national emergency and strike threats to win greater benefits. For example, William Hutcheson of the United Brotherhood of Carpenters and Joiners warned federal authorities that he would order union members to strike unless they were awarded closed-shop privileges on federal contract work. Despite repeated pledges by Gompers and other AFL leaders to cooperate with the war effort and to repudiate all strikes, spontaneous, unsanctioned walkouts remained the most common form of concerted wartime labor action.

As unemployment declined by 1918 to the lowest recorded level until then in United States history—1.4 percent—many workers improved their conditions simply by changing jobs. It was not unusual for workers to accept several jobs in a single day and then choose the most attractive one, or for annual factory turnover to climb over the 1000 percent level.

Between individuals changing jobs and workers collectively walking off the job, working conditions improved substantially. By 1919 almost half the country's workers had achieved the 48 hour week, and less than 26 percent toiled over 54 hours. Even before the National War Labor Board in the spring of 1918 instituted a basic eight-hour day on all war-contract work, over a million workers had already won the shorter day.

GOMPERS, THE AFL, AND THE WILSON ADMINISTRATION

American labor leaders intended to use prosperity, the war crisis atmosphere, and worker militancy to win added national influence for trade unionism. By cooperating fully with the national government in the war effort, Gompers and his associates in the AFL cemented their alliance with the Wilson Administration. AFL wartime policy implied no sudden shift in labor strategy. What it did mean, however, was a systematic effort to influence workers less enthusiastic about American foreign policy than their government officials and labor leaders.

Traditionally American labor leaders, though nonsocialist, had believed that wars were caused by capitalist competition for international markets and the drive for economic hegemony, the apparent case in World War I. The mass of American workers, like most citizens, moreover, opposed American involvement in Europe's fratricidal struggle. Ethnic factors also led millions of workers to oppose intervention overseas. German, Irish, and

Russian nationality workers were deeply skeptical about the Entente powers, especially Great Britain and Tsarist Russia. Equally important, many east Europeans had emigrated in part to escape conscription in their homelands. Even among American-born workers of British origins, before 1917 scarcely any enthusiasm for American intervention existed. No substantial sentiment stirred the working class in 1914-1915 to endorse American involvement in the war, an attitude then in harmony with Wilsonian policy and one that posed no problems for labor leaders in their relations with government officials.

Wilson and his advisers, however, were less committed to neutrality than the mass of workers, who, unlike high public officials, saw little connection between America's vital interests and the outcome of the European war. But Gompers as a result of his political alliance with the president, realized that Wilson might consider war preferable to sacrificing putative national interests, and so the AFL leader used his influence in the labor movement to combat antiwar factions among workers. Gompers's publicly avowed readiness in 1915 to support war, if it came, was probably not shared by most union members and workers, but he knew which way the political winds were blowing. Consequently it proved no surprise when Gompers endorsed Wilson's 1916 preparedness campaign, a policy roundly criticized by numerous labor and radical organizations. Late in that same year, Gompers linked the official labor movement more closely to government by accepting appointment as labor's representative to an advisory commission of a council of national defense. Finally in April 1917 Gompers and other AFL officials unhesitatingly supported Wilson's decision for war in a calculated effort to use patriotism to win respectability, status, and security for the labor movement.

Not all workers or their leaders, however, shared Gompers's devotion to Wilson and his belief in the righteousness of American intervention. Irish-American workers remained less than ecstatic about aiding the English. German-American workers were not always warm recruits in a war against the country of their origin. And Jewish-American workers reacted warily to a struggle which allied the United States to the Russia they had so recently fled. When these ethnic factors combined with socialist sentiments, open working-class opposition to Wilsonian diplomacy emerged. In Milwaukee, for example, an amalgam of ethnic and socialist supporters elected Victor Berger to Congress where he voiced sharp criticism of American participation in a capitalist war. A similar political milieu on New York City's Lower East Side produced Meyer London, a second socialist antiwar congressman.

Many of the antiwar workers, especially Jewish immigrant garment workers in New York City, joined with nonworking-class pacifists and radicals in an organized opposition to Wilsonian foreign policy. These antiwar workers formed the Workmen's Council—labor's adjunct to the People's Council for Peace and Democracy, the organization that united all those antiwar factions. The Workmen's Council, like its parent body and similar European left-wing antiwar groups, favored a policy of immediate peace based on no forcible annexations; no punitive indemnities; abolition of secret diplomacy; universal self-determination; disarmament; freedom of the seas; and arbitration of international disputes by tribunals. The Workman's Council moreover publicly endorsed the proposals for peace issued by the All-Russian Council of Workers and Soldiers Delegates (Soviet) and later endorsed by left-wing European socialists. In passing, it might be noted that many of Wilson's celebrated Fourteen Points were borrowed, perhaps stolen is the better word, outright from the antiwar left.

Rising popular opposition to the war, especially in Europe but also in America, vexed Wilson and threatened his objectives. Gompers, however, rushed to rescue the president from his quandary by rallying organized American workers around the flag. In June 1917, in a speech criticizing antiwar Jewish immigrants, he proclaimed: "This labor movement of ours is an American labor movement, not a Hebrew labor movement or a heathen labor movement." Later, with money, assistance, and advice provided by the Wilson Administration and its war propaganda minister, George Creel, Gompers founded the

American Alliance for Labor and Democracy, as the prowar competitor of the Workmen's Council. From first to last the American Alliance had its activities carefully orchestrated and closely supervised by Creel in Washington. Indeed it was little more than a government-conceived, -financed and -administered arrangement to attract working-class loyalty to the war effort, one that suggested that all opposition to Wilson was not only pro-German, but literally managed by German agents.

So well did Gompers perform his domestic patriotic duties that Wilson used him and other influential AFL trade-union leaders overseas. Wilson dispatched American trade-union missions abroad to accomplish United States diplomatic objectives. The President hoped that Gompers and his colleagues would stiffen the resolve of English, French, and Italian workers to fight the Germans and lessen the influence of antiwar left-wingers; Wilson also sent trade-union leaders to urge the Bolsheviks, who seized power in Russia in November 1917, to stay in the war. Ironically, Gompers loyally served the interests of the state department abroad by strengthening the hand of the European conservatives and rightists who in the end undermined Wilson's dreams of a liberal peace and a stable postwar world.

While the American Alliance promoted the war at home and Gompers spread the Wilsonian gospel overseas, events reconciled many previously antiwar workers to Wilson's foreign policy. First, Wilson's Fourteen Points Speech of January 1918 seemed to commit the president to the Workmen's Council's peace program. Second, the German offensive against Bolshevik Russia, culminating in the March 1918 Treaty of Brest-Litovsk, clearly identified Germany as the true enemy of left-wing socialists. As socialist Congressman Meyer London proclaimed on Labor Day, 1918: "There is no socialist in America, and for that matter, there is no socialist in the world, that would not like to see the defeat of German Kaiserism." Simultaneously, the previously antiwar journal of a garment workers' union now saw the conflict as "a war of emancipation in which labor joins hands with the president to lead the world to a new and better day."

In return for their support of Wilson's foreign policies, Gompers and other trade-union leaders expected to receive material compensation. True enough, appointments to prestigious international commissions conferred singular respectability and also immense ego satisfaction on American labor leaders. But union officials also represented a rank and file more concerned with wages and working conditions than with diplomatic missions. Moreover the influence that labor leaders had secured with the federal government flowed from their control of unions in a position to interfere with the war-production effort. Realistically these labor leaders knew that the best, perhaps only, means to continued influence was to increase total union membership. Hence AFL endorsement of Wilsonianism was founded on a clear expectation, indeed understanding, that federal officials would use their power to improve working conditions and promote trade unionism.

THE FEDERAL GOVERNMENT AND LABOR REFORM

Federal officials had their own compelling reasons for catering to working-class and trade-union interests. American war production administrators, preferring to benefit from European mistakes, did not wish to repeat the failures which had frustrated Britain's effort to rationalize the use of labor in the first year of the war. As we have seen, even before the United States declared war, Wilson had invited Gompers to serve on a special national committee charged with organizing domestic industrial production. And when war came in April 1917, more national defense production committees were established and more labor leaders appointed to serve on them. Particularly in such war-sensitive industries as shipbuilding, airplane production, and cantonment construction, the federal government created tripartite commissions composed of business, labor, and public representatives, and these commissions regulated wage rates, hours of labor and even the issue of union affiliation. The production codes they adopted later became a precedent for the industrial planning authorities of the New Deal era. In addition many influential prewar social reformers and also former socialists arrived in wartime Washington as ardent Wilsonians to serve their country. Proposals to promulgate national labor codes, to proclaim a national eight-hour day, and to sanction independent trade unionism, aims which had been unachievable, if not unthinkable, in peacetime, became a distinct possibility in wartime. The secretaries of war and labor, Newton D. Baker and William B. Wilson respectively, and such lesser but influential reformers in their departments as Walter Lippmann and Felix Frankfurter, promoted greater federal concern for the ordinary wage worker and open solicitude for the spread of trade unionism. For these federal officials, war had not only become the moral equivalent of reform; it also became the rationale for the introduction of sweeping national reforms. War, indeed, was fulfillment for some Progressive Americans.

But federal labor reforms came neither easily nor immediately. As we have seen, during the initial six months after American intervention, discontented rank-and-file workers initiated an unprecedented wave of strikes. Strikers interfered with the production of copper, lumber, and food grains, all items vital to the war effort. All these strikes dismayed Wilson but none so much as the industrial conflicts in copper and lumber. In most industrial disputes the president could rely on assistance from official AFL leaders to urge workers to return to the job. But the walkouts in copper and lumber were sponsored by the IWW, which had publicly repudiated the war and Wilsonianism. Worse yet, the IWW strikes, mostly in Rocky Mountain and Pacific Northwest states, had caused incidents of labor repression unprecedented in American history. At a time when Wilson portrayed the war as a struggle for democracy and liberty, mine owners and their allies in Bisbee, Arizona in July 1917 summarily deported 1100 workers from their homes and families in order to break a strike and smash organized labor in Arizona. At the end of the month, vigilantes in the copper mining center of Butte, Montana, kidnapped and lynched IWW agitator Frank Little. Simultaneously in the woods of Washington and Oregon and the oil fields of Kansas and Oklahoma vigilantes and local law officers destroyed IWW offices and savagely beat individual

Wobblies. How could Wilson ask American workers to sacrifice their own or their sons' lives to defeat German autocracy abroad when copper and lumber barons built industrial tyrannies at home? Moreover, if employers could use violence to smash strikes by allegedly radical antiwar unions, would they not tend to use similar tactics against AFL unions and prowar workers? The latter possibility deeply troubled Gompers and several of the social reformers influential in the war and labor departments.

Tripartite boards worked to preserve labor-management harmony, or so it seemed, in industries where employers had previously practiced collective bargaining and where strong craft unions functioned, but not in such industries as copper and lumber or the basic mass-production sector where employers refused to bargain with unions and the AFL lacked members. Gompers, however, suggested a solution to wartime strike problems that President Wilson implemented. In August 1917, Gompers proposed that the president appoint a special commission to investigate those sectors of the economy plagued by labor discontent and industrial conflict. Wilson promptly appointed a federal commission. The president's Mediation Commission, as it was known, was chaired by former trade unionist and now secretary of labor William B. Wilson, and it included two businessmen sympathetic to labor unionism and two AFL officials. Equally important, its secretary and real policymaker, Felix Frankfurter, was committed to promoting "responsible" unionism of the AFL variety, and used his considerable influence to do so.

The Mediation Commission investigated strikes in the Arizona copper mines, the Washington State forests, the Pacific Coast telephone industry, and the Chicago packing industry. In all these disputes, it proposed consistent general policies and specific suggestions for industrial peace. The commission's guiding principle was the belief that workers had as much right to organized representation as their employers and that workers must be protected against the arbitrary exercise of corporate power. This principle implied recognition of AFL unions where they had members and the creation of grievance boards where "responsible" unionism was absent. In return for the employers' recognition of AFL unions and the establishment of grievance boards, the commission promised to help remove the "disloyal, subversive" IWW from the copper and lumber industries. With the IWW threat once removed, employers had less reason to respond to their workers' demands, and so, the more successful the commission proved in purging the Wobblies the less successful it was in promoting AFL affiliates or in protecting the worker's interests. The commission's activities and reports made evident the relationship between labor militancy and federal solicitude for the worker. When strikes crippled full production, federal concern for industrial justice rose. When rank-and-file militancy declined, federal interest in decent working conditions fell precipitously.

Although the Mediation Commission had some success in restoring peace to the industries it investigated, its proposals remained merely advisory and hence unenforceable. Not only that, but different branches of the federal government pursued conflicting labor policies. The labor department encouraged unionism; the commerce department resisted it; industrialists serving on wartime commissions insisted that the emergency *must not* be used to change preexisting labor-management relations; their union counterparts asserted that workers deserved trade unions of their own choosing and a more democratic system of industrial relations; and the president seemed isolated from the implementation of wartime labor policies. As strikes continued to disrupt production and federal policies toward labor fluctuated erratically, many reform-minded officials and labor leaders urged the president to enunciate a more orderly and systematic national labor policy. Thus, in January 1918, President Wilson authorized his secretary of labor to systematize federal policies. Secretary Wilson created a War Labor Conference Board composed of five representatives from business and five from labor (they, in turn, chose two public representatives to chair the board). He charged the new board with recommending labor policies to be implemented by the federal government. It did so in March. Basically it accepted the principles of labor relations previously enunciated by the President's Mediation Commission, recommending the appointment of a new federal agency to enforce them. Following those recommendations, President Wilson in April 1918 established the National War Labor Board (NWLB).

The labor relations principles and policies adopted by the NWLB demanded a total suspension of strikes and lockouts for the duration of the war; that employers recognize the right of workers to join independent trade unions and bargain collectively with those unions; that industries establish a basic eight-hour day; that wages be fixed in accordance with prevailing local standards; that women receive equal pay; and that there be no alteration in the status of nonunion shops without the employer's consent. Acting on these principles, the board promoted union growth where labor organizations had footholds and it obtained improved working conditions and higher wages for millions of unorganized workers.

Between January 1, 1917 and January 1, 1919, trade-union membership climbed from 2,370,000 to 3,260,000, and a little later rose to about four million. The board also played an important role in the AFL's unionization of the Chicago packinghouses in 1918 and in an AFL campaign to organize the steelworkers. As William Z. Foster, the leader of the organizing campaigns in meatpacking and steel industries, observed: " ... the Federal administration was friendly; the right to organize was freely conceded by the government and even insisted upon.... The gods were indeed fighting on the side of Labor." Or as a member of the Railway Carmen's Union added: "A worker... with a union card in his pocket will be looked after and has been assured by the government of this great country of ours that he will get a square deal." But in August 1919, with the war then ten months over, the War Labor Board was suspended, just when it was most needed, as we shall see, in a time of unsurpassed labor militancy and crisis.

Yet beneath the tangible rewards labor won from government and employers during the war lurked more sinister, and in the end, more triumphant forces. For the strengthened institutions of government, which were used to promote AFL-type unionism and extensive social reform, could also be turned to less desirable ends. The same government propagandists who praised the contribution of workers and their unions to the war effort also spread the notion that any criticism of Wilson and the war was tantamount to serving Imperial Germany; indeed, propagandists went as far as to suggest that all critics of the war were in the pay of the German government, which initiated a new form of gold rush—the frantic search to locate the Kaiser's coins clinking in the pockets of antiwar Americans. Not only did criticism of Wilson create suspicion of German influence; simply to be an immigrant from Germany or one of her allies brought one under suspicion and sometimes outright attack. When the Bolsheviks seized power in Russia in November 1917, fear of communism was added to the dread of German imperialism. And just as numerous reformers and lesser federal bureaucrats used the crisis to secure liberal social changes, many private citizens and public officials used the war to solidify the existing distribution of social and economic power.

Socialists and Wobblies, in particular, felt the full weight of subversive-hunting bureaucrats and citizen vigilantes. The justice department and the post office department practically eliminated the Socialist party from its remaining nonurban strongholds. Denied the right to use the mails to distribute literature and with their leaders either arrested or hunted by federal agents, socialists in such places as Kansas, Oklahoma, the Dakotas, and Washington State watched their locals atrophy. Prominent spokesmen for the national party did not go untouched. Victor Berger, the socialist congressman from Milwaukee, and Eugene Debs, the personification of American socialism, were convicted and imprisoned on charges of sedition. Along with them, numerous less prominent but equally antiwar or anti-Wilson socialists went to federal prisons. A once thriving and buoyant socialist movement never recovered from wartime repression, and the process of decay set in motion by government witchhunters was completed after 1919 by left-wing sectarianism, the most notable example of which was the establishment in America in 1919 of two rival communist parties.

But Socialists fared well compared to Wobblies—and for good reason. Political socialists scarcely presented more than a rhetorical threat to Wilsonianism; the Wobblies, by virtue of their militant organizing and strikes, posed a direct threat to the war effort. Federal authorities eventually used every means at their disposal to thwart the IWW menace. Early in 1917 federal troops broke IWW-sponsored strikes, and justice department agents infiltrated the organization as spies. The federal government also allowed, sometimes encouraged, the governors of the various western states threatened by the Wobblies to turn to outright repression. Some public officials were not above suggesting the use of concentration camps. When vigilante groups summarily punished suspected Wobblies, local, state, and federal authorities seldom obstructed or punished such extralegal action. In fact, one of the most favored lines of argument used by government legal advisers was the concept that public officials should suppress the IWW without heed to due process in order to put the vigilantes out of business.

Finally, when all these repressive actions proved less than satisfactory in curbing the Wobblies, the federal government took the final step. On September 5, 1917, justice department agents raided the halls and headquarters of the IWW. They seized everything they could lay their hands on, including the love letters of IWW editor Ralph Chaplin. Soon thereafter, federal grand juries in Chicago, Omaha, Wichita, Sacramento, and Fresno produced indictments against almost the entire first- and second-line leadership of the IWW, charging the more than 200 indicted labor leaders with various acts of espionage and sedition. The indictments were followed in turn by a series of political trials, the most notable being held in Chicago and Sacramento, at which the indicted Wobblies were convicted and received stiff sentences.

The law had in the case of the Wobblies proved to be an effective instrument of repression. When the justice department observed the formal requirements of legal due process—whatever the actual substance of the proceedings may have been—the American conscience rested easy as radicals received their due. Where courtroom charades seemed too costly or time-consuming, federal officials used summary Immigration Service procedures to deport alien or naturalized Wobblies. Federal repression changed the whole basis of the IWW's existence. Before September 1917 the IWW seemed a flourishing labor organization, daily gaining recruits and funds; afterwards its leaders were imprisoned, its ranks decimated, and its treasury depleted by legal expenses. A once fighting labor organization had been transformed into a legal-defense agency, spending its slender resources combating writs, government lawyers, and judges, a struggle from which there was no surcease.

To make sense of wartime federal labor policies was difficult, as one critic and social reformer observed. "Here," he noted, "were three branches of the federal government pursuing three radically diverging and hopelessly conflicting policies towards the wage workers at the very moment when the nation was making patriotic appeal to the workers to get out a maximum production.... The United States Department of Justice was arresting them, the President's Mediation Committee was telling them that they must organize into unions, and the United States Supreme Court was announcing that if they attempted to organize under certain conditions they would be guilty of contempt of court."

Despite unprecedented rank-and-file militancy and singular federal solicitude for organized labor, unions scarcely thwarted the war effort, nor did President Wilson truckle to labor.

For all the ambiguity, and even deceit, inherent in wartime federal labor policy, the AFL and the trade unions emerged from the crisis stronger than ever. Labor had earned social respectability and status; it had become a partner, albeit a junior one, in the alliance between big business and government. Gompers and other trade-union leaders not only sat in the councils of national power; they also represented the United States abroad. Never had the future appeared so bright for the American labor movement.

The impact of war and federal labor policies on union membership, wage rates, hours of labor, and industrial safety can be measured. More important but less subject to precise measurement was war's impact on the consciousness of American workers. The vast propaganda machine built by the federal government stressed to workers how much their labor meant to the nation's security and future. Government propagandists regularly reminded the nation's workers that war was being waged not only to spread political democracy overseas, but also to widen industrial democracy at home. Workers were reminded that without their full contribution to the war effort, allied armies in the field could not prevail. Not surprisingly, private employers, short of labor and eager for increased productivity and the higher profits that went with it, joined in extolling the virtues of American workers. In such industries as steel, employers aggressively Americanized their immigrant labor force, encouraging aliens to become citizens.

For two years workers heard and read tributes to their importance and virtues. They were the backbone of society, their dedication and willingness to work without limit would make the world safe for democracy and, as Lloyd George put it in England, their own country a land fit for heroes to live in. Was it thus any wonder that immigrant steelworkers suddenly took a new and militant interest in trade unionism and the establishment of industrial democracy? Or that the immigrant leader of a union of immigrant clothing workers, Sidney Hillman, announcing that the nation stood on the threshold of a new social era, proclaimed: "What labor is demanding all over the world today is not a few material things like more dollars and fewer hours of work, but a right to a voice in the conduct of industry." Or as the liberal journal *The New Republic* put it: "We have already passed to a new era, the transition to a state in which labor will be the predominating element."

Some labor leaders, like Hillman, were even fired with messianic dreams, as the following letter to his daughter reveals: "As I was looking in their eyes . . . I could not resist, I told them what they wanted to hear—that their Day is at hand, Messiah is arriving. He may be with us any minute—one can hear the footsteps of the Deliverer—if only he listens intently. Labor will rule and the World will be free. And as I was telling them these words, a new fire kindled in their eyes—the fire of hope, will and determination. A thrill went through me at this time—I was watching them and behold, a wonderful change took place. At first I only felt his presence and then I actually saw him in all his wonderful majesty—strong—determined, full of love. The Champion was with us in the Hall, ready to do battle. The people—an awakened people—"

ANNUS MIRABILIS: 1919

In 1919, Hillman's Messiah indeed seemed at hand. Revolutionaries and revolutions appeared in the ascendant. The Bolsheviks by then had held power in Russia for two years, despite domestic counterrevolutionaries and foreign invaders; Bela Kun's communist regime had seized power in Hungary; communists threatened to capture hegemony inside postwar Germany; the British Labour Party had announced its Programme for a Socialist Postwar Order, and it had replaced the Liberal Party as that nation's second national party; in Italy workers seized factories. Wherever one turned, the United States not excepted, one saw turmoil and the masses in motion.

The year 1919 began in the United States with a general strike in the city of Seattle. For five days the city's organized workers paralyzed all local industry and services, except for those items essential to life and health. In a remarkable demonstration of administrative skill and good sense, Seattle labor maintained stability and vital services in the city. Nevertheless local conservatives led by Mayor Ole Hanson condemned the strikers as Bolsheviks and anarchists and soon initiated a Red-hunt.

Seattle was only the beginning of an unprecedented wave of labor unrest. Over four million workers participated in strikes in 1919, a number never before reached and not to be exceeded until 1946. Strikers demanded shorter hours, wage increases to catch up with wartime inflation, union recognition, and even freedom for Tom Mooney and wartime political prisoners. In the fall of 1919 over 300,000 soft-coal miners walked out of the pits in defiance of the federal government and court injunctions. Only a direct plea from President Wilson to UMW president John L. Lewis induced him to call off the strike. Even then, rank-and-file miners proved recalcitrant, and they later voted that their union seek the nationalization of the nation's coal mines. Boston's police force struck in 1919 in order to obtain union recognition, and their walkout opened the city to several days of looting and crime, once more raising the spectre of Bolshevism loose in the land. Immigrant textile workers paralyzed industry in Lawrence, Massachusetts, as they had in 1912, and again under radical leadership, this time coming from A. J. Muste. Railroad workers, who did not strike in 1919, nevertheless endorsed government ownership of the railroads, a position they ratified the following year when a coalition of sixteen unions representing 1,850,000 members decided by a 90 percent membership vote to strike if Congress failed to enact the Plumb Plan for nationalization of the railroads. As working-class militancy spread, union membership soared by early 1920 to over five million.

Working-class politics also assumed new dimensions. In Chicago and Illinois under the leadership of John Fitzpatrick, so-called labor progressives formed a citywide labor party which they expanded into a statewide organization and finally into a National Labor Party created to participate in the 1920 presidential election. Similar labor party movements arose in New York and in other industrial cities scattered across the nation. Immigrant workers, moreover, had begun to swell the ranks of the Socialist party's Foreign Language Federations as early as 1917, and by 1919 they had become the party's dominant numerical faction, strong enough to break away from reformist socialism and unite with other Bolshevik sympathizers to form an American communist movement. Equally ominous, the spring and summer of 1919 witnessed what appeared to worried citizens to be the onset of an anarchist murder campaign. Such famous business and public officials as John D. Rockefeller, Jr., Mayor Ole Hanson, and United States Attorney General A. Mitchell Palmer had bombs mailed to them.

If all this were not enough to cause anxiety, on September 22, 1919 more than three hundred thousand steelworkers stopped working as part of an AFL drive to organize the steel industry.

Since the defeat of the Amalgamated Association of Iron and Steel Workers at Homestead in 1892, the steel industry had become impregnable to unionism. But the war opened steel to unionism. Mass immigration ended, and steel companies could no longer replace discontented workers with armies of new immigrants. Moreover, wartime propaganda and Americanization programs led immigrant workers to become citizens with a permanent stake in their adopted country. They also began to see that autocracy was as unacceptable in the workplace as in the political world. Finally, during the war the federal government encouraged the spread of "responsible" AFL-type unionism. All these factors led the AFL executive council to agree in 1918 to sanction a campaign to organize the steel industry.

Under the direction of William Z. Foster, a former Wobbly, successful wartime organizer of the Chicago stockyards, and later Communist party leader, some twenty-four separate craft unions pooled their resources and manpower in a National Committee for Organizing Iron and Steel Workers; each of these unions found some workers in the industry over whom they claimed jurisdictional rights, with all residual jurisdictional claims falling to the Amalgamated Association. Clumsy as this device may seem, it was the AFL's response to demands for industrial unionism and the only response the executive council would sanction.

During the summer of 1918, Foster's National Committee made substantial headway among steelworkers. Immigrant workers, in particular, rushed to join the union. The response to the campaign far surpassed what many of the timid craft union leaders had expected. In area after area of the industry, rank-and-file militancy outran leadership control. While the war continued, the steel companies were reduced to fighting a rearguard action against the unions. But when the war unexpectedly ended in November 1918 labor had not yet completed its basic organizing work, nor had it won union recognition from employers; employers, however, were now free to take the offensive against the unions.

With war over and the National War Labor Board disbanded, a strike in the steel industry became inevitable. Bereft of federal guardianship, the Organizing Committee, on the one hand, could not callously cast adrift the thousands of workers who still looked to it for assistance. Liberated from government wartime restraints, the steel barons, on the other hand, felt free to smash the union drive. Every union effort to meet with employers was coldly rebuffed. The only negotiations that occurred were between employers and President Wilson, and labor leaders and Wilson, with the labor leaders looking to the president to coax employers into negotiations with labor. But the only assistance Wilson offered labor was advice to forego a strike until the President's Industrial Conference met in Washington in October to discuss postwar industrial and labor relations. Meantime, however, the steel companies discharged known union members and conducted a widespread antiunion propaganda campaign. If the National Committee postponed a strike at the president's behest, it might find itself without any members employed in the steel industry. The choice for the union members had become simple: to submit without a struggle or fight for what steel-workers desired.

And so the strike came. As it unfolded over the course of the next three months, it revealed with perfect clarity the weakness of organized labor compared to corporate capital. Employers, following traditional practices, pitted American-born against foreign-born workers and blacks against whites. For good reasons, the thousands of blacks recruited as workers during the war and the thousands more added during the strike proved antipathetic to unions and excellent strikebreakers. In communities where their power was unchallenged employers denied free speech, press, and assembly to union members; they also used local police, deputies, and judges to keep the union out. The steel companies unleashed a national propaganda barrage that portrayed most steelworkers as content with their jobs and which accused union organizers and strike leaders of serving Bolshevik masters eager to revolutionize American society. The whole antistrike campaign was conducted systematically and with a singleness of purpose. Against this, the best that organized labor could offer was an internally divided Organizing Committee, many of whose affiliates refused to contribute money or men. And so the strike was lost, signifying, as Thomas Brooks has observed, "the end of labor's wartime fortunes, ... the weakness of the protection afforded labor by the Wilson Administration, and ... an employer offensive that set back the labor movement for a generation." They also discovered, as David Brody has noted, that "depending on their own economic strength, American workers could not defeat the massed power of open-shop industry."

The defeat of the steelworkers coincided with an intense period of domestic reaction against the idealistic goals associated with Wilson's crusade to make the world safe for democracy. With the aid of Gompers and the AFL, Wilson had secured the world from German hegemony, but he had not made it safe for radicalism, revolution, or even for some small advances in democracy. As labor leaders learned during the Great Steel Strike of 1919, the propaganda devices developed against Germany during the war could just as easily be turned against disturbers of the domestic peace.

LABOR AND NORMALCY

As the American people prepared to return to "normalcy" in 1920, they confronted a mature industrial society. For the first time in the history of the nation, reported the 1920 census, urban population outstripped rural population. The blue-collar labor force in the primary industries—manufacturing, mining, and logging—had reached a peak it would not again touch or exceed except for a brief period during World War II. Proportionate to the total work force, fewer Americans than ever were self-employed, and fewer people worked on the nation's farms. By 1920, the typical worker was a semiskilled machine operator who labored for wages in the mass-production industries—autos, electrical goods, and petrochemicals—which would characterize the economy of the 1920s. In almost all sectors of the economy, except for the building and printing trades, the highly skilled artisans and craftsmen who in the 1870s and 1880s had set the pace of work, controlled the actual process of production, and monopolized the secrets of their trade, were a disappearing breed. They had been replaced by more efficient machines or seen their singular skills diluted and parceled out among less skilled but more specialized workers by scientific managers educated in the nation's thriving engineering schools.

By 1920 the working class had also assumed its basic ethnoreligious structure. Unrestricted immigration would end temporarily in 1921 and permanently in 1924. Catholic immigrants from the east and south of Europe formed the bulk of the nation's blue-collar machine operators in the nation's heavy industries and in northern and western mines. In the South, American-born white men and women, many of whom were recent migrants from a declining countryside, filled the region's thriving textile mills and also its coal mines. Everywhere nonwhites and women rounded out the ranks of the least skilled and lowest paid industrial workers. American-born workers and North European immigrants continued to dominate the skilled hierarchies and positions as foremen and supervisors.

Fifty years of industrial history had taught workers the importance of organization and collective action. The experience of World War I had intensified militancy, solidarity, and the organizational impulse among American workers, who increasingly resorted to collective action in order to control better their jobs and lives. Nothing better illustrated the growth of militancy and the desire for union organization than the extent of wartime strikes and the extraordinary labor outburst in 1919. In 1920, over five million workers belonged to unions, more than doubling the size of the prewar organized labor force.

But growth in the size of organized labor and increased militancy among workers in 1919 cloaked basic weaknesses in trade unionism, which had emerged during the 1919 strikes and which would become clearer in the 1920s. Ethnic and racial divisions continued to undermine working-class solidarity. The East St. Louis "race riot" of 1917 indicated how easy it was to turn white workers against black ones when they competed for jobs and housing. Chicago's bloody "race riot" of 1919 had its origins, among other sources, in black and white competition for jobs, a competition which helped wreck unionism in the meatpacking industry. The "Great Steel Strike" also ignited ethnic and racial conflicts among workers. American-born skilled workers tended to support their employers and accuse immigrant strikers of "un-American" radicalism, while blacks served by the thousands as strikebreakers. Not only did ethnic and racial factors still vitiate working-class solidarity in 1920, but organized labor remained excluded from the nation's basic industries. Indeed, as the 1920s progressed, the few union footholds in basic industry, especially coal mining, would loosen. Only those workers who still commanded irreplaceable skills and labored for smaller employers, as did building tradesmen and printers, for example, belonged to effective unions which grew in size and power even during the 1920s. Ironically, by the end of the decade, when the United States was the most powerful and mature industrial economy in the world, its organized labor force was more elitist in composition than when Engels had first commented in the 1880s on the "aristocratic" character of American trade unionism.

"Normalcy" in the United States meant a basic disparity in organization and power between workers and their employers, particularly in the mass-production industries and in smaller industrial communities where the business class exercised economic and social hegemony. Postwar government attitudes and actions, as presaged by Wilson's antiunion actions in the 1919 steel strike, boded ill for the future of organized labor. By 1920 the stage had been well set for the welfare capitalism and managerial autocracy which would dominate labor relations throughout the 1920s.

Not surprisingly, then, when sociologists Robert and Helen Lynd investigated Muncie, Indiana in the mid-1920s in order to analyze the social structure and processes of an American industrial city (*Middletown* [1929]), they were struck by the enormous gulf in attitudes and behavior separating local businessmen from workers. The businessmen were joiners socially and economically; they were proud of their activities, vigorous in their control of local society, and certain that the future would extend their influence and power. Workers, mostly American-born Protestants, however, existed in a lonelier world devoid of social and economic institutions outside the family; they took little pride in their jobs, felt themselves impotent in local affairs, and looked to the future with as much foreboding as hope. Despite their bleak community lives, perhaps because of them, Muncie's workers evinced no class consciousness, nor did they favor trade unionism. And so it would remain, until the Great Depression and the coming of the New Deal.

Bibliographical Essay

This brief summary of the literature in the field intends neither to duplicate nor to compete with the incredibly complete and up-to-date bibliography put together by Maurice F. Neufeld, Daniel J. Leab, and Dorothy Swanson in *American Working Class History: A Representative Bibliography* (New York, 1983). That bibliography can also be supplemented by the bibliographies which appear annually in *Labor History* (the leading scholarly journal in the field since 1959) and *International Labor and Working Class History* (ILWCH), which since the mid-1970s has published excellent review-essays and guides to current research in the field. In the following commentary I intend to focus on what have become the two dominant approaches to the study of labor history, to suggest their respective merits, and to consider the absence of what might be called a new synthesis for the field.

Historians commonly work primarily with the written record of the past, and this custom has had an obvious impact on the content of history. Individual workingmen and women ordinarily did not keep diaries, write memoirs, or merit biographies. The more common and respectable their lives the more obscure they were to their own contemporaries as well as to subsequent generations of historians. The ordinary and typical, perhaps the substance of most sociology, has seldom attracted the interest of historians eager to recreate the excitement or drama of the past. Especially has this been so when written sources are rare, a factor which had caused most historians to neglect the working class.

Not so the history of organized labor movements, working-class political parties, protest movements, and industrial conflicts. All these institutions and phenomena either maintained their own archives or were written about extensively, providing a vast body of sources in which future scholars might later dig. And so trade unions, left-wing political movements, and notable industrial conflicts have attracted their share of historians.

Two massive multivolume studies cover thoroughly the ground of traditional labor history. Conceived some three decades apart and the products of diametrically opposed ideological perspectives, the two histories ironically resemble each other in many ways. John R. Commons et al., in their classic, *History of Labor in the United States,* 4 vols., (New York, 1918–1935), especially vols. 2–4, examine the maturation of American trade unionism, a movement which, according to the several authors, evolved necessarily from the impractical, utopian, anti-wage-system beliefs of the Jacksonian and post–Civil War labor movements to the practical, businesslike, nonradical labor movement of Samuel Gompers and the AFL. For Commons et al., the "bread and butter" trade unions served as an effective substitute for Frederick Jackson Turner's vanishing frontier in maintaining interclass harmony, social stability, and democratic order. The most brilliant distillation of this approach to American labor history, one which sought to transform principles derived from the history of American trade unionism into a universal theory, is by an associate and student of Commons, Selig Perlman. Perlman's *Theory of the Labor Movement* (New York, 1928), despite substantial flaws, deserves to be read and reread as the only full-blown attempt to fit American trade-union history into a larger theoretical framework. Indeed, any student interested in either the trade-union or political manifestations of American working-class history must begin his or her intellectual journey with the writings of Commons and Perlman.

Also perceiving American trade-union history as the inevitable progression from utopian, nonclass-conscious organizations to "progressive," realistic unions is Philip S. Foner, *History of the Labor Movement in the United States,* 6 vols. (New York, 1947-1983). The work of this most prolific of American Marxist historians scarcely differs from that of Commons in detail or scope. Foner simply reverses values and terms of reference. He praises the anticapitalists and damns the advocates of labor-capital accommodation.

But stripped of their excess ideological baggage which, in the case of Commons is implicit and in Foner's case explicit, these two multivolume histories agree about what factors labor historians should investigate: trade unions, left-wing political parties, employer labor policies, government-labor interactions, and industrial conflicts.

For a traditional form of general labor history but one which diverges at many points from Commons-Perlman and Foner, one might examine Robert H. Hoxie, *A History of Trade Unionism in the United States* (1917). This book presents interesting analyses of what Hoxie labels "business," "reform," and "revolutionary" unionism. Equally interesting, especially as a variation of sorts on Perlman's *Theory*, is Frank Tannenbaum, *A Philosophy of Labor* (New York, 1951).

The history of trade unions as institutions has long attracted the interest of labor economists, many of whom beginning early in the century wrote studies of individual unions still worth reading. Among the best in that group one might include Jacob Hollander, *Studies in American Trade Unionism* (New York, 1906); George Barnett, *The Printers: A Study in American Trade Unionism* (Cambridge, Mass., 1909) and *Chapters on Machinery and Labor* (Carbondale, Ill., 1969 ed.); Jesse S. Robinson, *The Amalgamated Association of Iron, Steel, and Tin Workers* (Baltimore, 1920); Norman Ware, *The Labor Movement in the United States, 1860-1895* (New York, 1929), remains a classic. Two fine older books also treat the history of organized workers during World War I: Alexander Bing, *War Time Strikes and Their Adjustment* (New York, 1921) and Gordon S. Watkins, *Labor Problems and Labor Administration in the U.S. During the World War* (Urbana, Ill., 1920). On this topic one must now also consult Valerie Jean Connor, *The National War Labor Board: Stability, Social Justice, and the Voluntary State in World War I* (Chapel Hill, N.C., 1983).

The attraction of the institutional approach for historians and labor economists has never diminished. Harvard University Press, for example, has been publishing a series of institutional labor histories among which the best have been: David Brody, *The Butcher Workmen: A Study of Unionization* (1964) and Lloyd Ulman, *The Rise of the National Trade Union* (1955), which analyze the evolution of union structure as determined by technological change, the composition of the work force, and the dynamics of the national economy. Other volumes in the series— Mark Perlman, *The Machinists: A New Study in American Trade Unionism* (1961); Garth L. Mangum, *The Operating Engineers: The Economic History of a Trade Union* (1964); Martin Segal, *The Rise of the United Association: National Unionism in the Pipe Trade, 1884-1924* (1970); Fred C. Munson, *History of the Lithographers Union* (1963); and Joseph P. Goldberg, *The Maritime Story: A Study of Labor Relations* (1958)—all detail fully the internal constitutional and structural evolution of the unions examined but they barely relate the world of the workers and their unions to the broader historical context of American society. The most recent volume in this series, one true to the traditions and style of its predecessors, appeared in

1983: Walter Galenson, *The United Brotherhood of Carpenters* (Cambridge, Mass., 1983).

Two studies intended to be noninstitutional in their analysis of the American labor movement—Gerald Grob, *Workers and Utopia: A Study of Ideological Conflict in the American Labor Movement, 1865-1900* (Evanston, Ill., 1961) and Milton Derber, *The American Idea of Industrial Democracy, 1865-1965* (Urbana, 1970)—in fact play a simple variation on the Commons-Foner institutional approach. Grob and Derber focus on ideology, not institutions, but they, too, describe the triumph of practical, businesslike, "middle class" notions of consensus, accommodation, and democracy over more utopian, radical, and "un-American" concepts of conflict. Even Victor Greene in his revealing and rewarding study of an immigrant working-class group—*The Slavic Community on Strike: Immigrant Labor in Anthracite Pennsylvania* (South Bend, 1968)—chose to refight an old problem raised by Commons: whether or not immigrant workers were organizable. And finally, Philip Taft's *The AFL in the Time of Gompers* (New York, 1957) and *Organized Labor in American History* (New York, 1964) rework the Commons-Perlman version of labor history in a dull encyclopedic manner. Moreover, most of these scholars, except for Brody and Greene, tend to characterize labor organizations *a priori* as "regressive" (reactionary or utopian) or "progressive" (AFL types).

Some of the institutional union histories, especially those written by historians rather than labor economists, have never lost sight of the broader historical context. Among the best in that category are: Robert A. Christie, *Empire in Wood: A History of the United Brotherhood of Carpenters and Joiners of America* (Ithaca, N.Y., 1956); Richard Lingenfelter, *The Hardrock Miners: A History of the Mining Labor Movement in the American West, 1863-1893* (Berkeley, 1974); Mark Wyman, *Hard Rock Epic: Western Miners and the Industrial Revolution, 1860-1910* (Berkeley, 1979); Robert Ozanne, *A Century of Labor-Management Relations at McCormick and International Harvester* (Madison, 1967); Cletus Daniel, *Bitter Harvest: A History of California Farmworkers, 1870-1941* (Ithaca, N.Y.,

1981); and for a slightly different slant on the history of unions, Warren Van Tine, *The Making of the Labor Bureaucrat: Union Leadership in the United States, 1870-1920* (Amherst, Mass., 1973).

Studies of working-class politics have traditionally fallen into the same pattern. The focus has been on the actions of organized labor groups and third parties, not the behavior of masses of workers. At that level there is little to add to Chester M. Destler's collection of essays on late nineteenth-century protest politics and farmer-labor radicalism, *American Radicalism, 1865-1901* (Ithaca, 1946); Howard H. Quint's encyclopedic history of the origins of American socialism, *The Forging of American Socialism* (Columbia, S.C., 1953); David Shannon's valuable and succinct summary of twentieth-century socialism, as reflected in the inner history of the Socialist Party of America, *The Socialist Party of America* (New York, 1955); Marc Karson's detailed analysis of the political activities of the AFL which includes an interesting long chapter probing Roman Catholic influence in the labor movement, *American Labor Unions and Politics, 1900-1918* (Carbondale, Ill., 1958); John H. M. Laslett's suggestive study of the changing political sympathies and the decline of radicalism in six national trade unions, *Labor and the Left: A Study of Socialist and Radical Influence in the American Labor Movement, 1881-1924* (New York, 1970); and James Weinstein's revisionist *The Decline of Socialism in America, 1912-1925* (New York, 1967). With the exception of Weinstein, all these historians explain the American labor movement's rejection of socialism and socialism's failure in the United States in terms derived from the findings and theories of Commons and Perlman as modified and elaborated by Louis Hartz's statement of American exceptionalism, *The Liberal Tradition in America* (New York, 1955).

More recently, however, several studies of labor radicalism and socialism have added more dimension and complexity to the story. For efforts to relate the history of the IWW to broader currents in American history, one should consult Melvyn Dubofsky, *We Shall Be All: A History of the IWW* (Chicago,

1969), and Joseph R. Conlin, *Bread and Roses Too: Studies of the Wobblies* (Westport, Conn., 1969), and *At the Point of Production: The Local History of the I.W.W.* (Westport, Conn., 1981). Two controversial books which treat the relationship between Populism and labor are Norman Pollack, *The Populist Response to Industrial America* (Cambridge, Mass., 1962) and Lawrence Goodwyn, *Democratic Promise: The Populist Movement in America* (New York, 1976). Two other studies follow the evolution of radical politics from Populism through socialism in the Southwest and the Pacific Northwest: James R. Green, *Grass-Roots Socialism: Radical Movements in the Southwest, 1895–1943* (Baton Rouge, 1978); and Carlos A. Schwantes, *Radical Heritage: Labor, Socialism, and Reform in Washington and British Columbia, 1885–1917* (Seattle, 1979). A collection of essays edited by Seymour Martin Lipset and John H. M. Laslett, *Failure of a Dream?* (Berkeley, 1984 ed.) provides conflicting evaluations of the role and impact of radicals in American history. Aileen S. Kraditor's *The Radical Persuasion: 1890–1917* (Baton Rouge, 1981) is an idiosyncratic intellectual history which tries to use the findings of the "new" social and labor history to condemn past radicals as incipient totalitarians. Finally, one might take note of a study of more conventional labor politics: Gary M. Fink, *Labor's Search for Political Order: The Political Behavior of the Missouri Labor Movement, 1890–1940* (Columbia, Mo., 1973).

Also lending weight to the Commons-Perlman version of American labor history are several biographies of notable trade-union leaders. The following are among the best: Jonathan Grossman, *William Sylvis: Pioneer of American Labor* (New York, 1945), a sympathetic portrait of the post–Civil War labor leader; Bernard Mandel, *Samuel Gompers* (Yellow Springs, Ohio, 1963), written from the perspective of a Marxist who praises Gompers for his youthful radical failures and damns him for his mature "pragmatic" achievements; Elsie Gluck, *John Mitchell, Miner: Labor's Bargain with the Gilded Age* (New York, 1929), an understanding but critical study of what the author sees as "class collaboration"; and Hyman Weintraub's

Andrew Furuseth: Emancipator of the Seamen (Berkeley, 1959), a revealing account of trade-union history on the Pacific Coast, and a labor leader who combined militancy, social conservatism and radicalism. The student, however, should not rely on these biographies, for several autobiographies offer revealing glimpses into the psyches and policies of American labor leaders. No one can really comprehend the labor history of the late nineteenth century without first encountering the conscious and unconscious self-deceptions and rationalizations presented by Terence Powderly in *The Path I Trod* (New York, 1947) and *Thirty Years of Labor* (Columbus, Ohio, 1889), and Samuel Gompers, *Seventy Years of Life and Labor,* 2 vols. (New York, 1925). William D. Haywood, *Bill Haywood's Book* (New York, 1929), strikingly reveals how fundamental American myths can be put to radical use. Excellent for its insights into life and culture in turn-of-the-century mining camps is John O. H. P. Hall, ed., *John Brophy: A Miner's Life* (Madison, Wis., 1964). In a class by itself because it delves into the yearnings, self-doubts, cultural values, and sexual drives of an immigrant worker and later labor leader, and also because it was not intended for publication, is Abraham Bisno, *Abraham Bisno: Union Pioneer* (Madison, Wis., 1967). Several recent biographical studies provide new and stimulating slants which revise firmly held beliefs about the lives of their subjects. Stuart B. Kaufman, *Samuel Gompers and the Origins of the AFL* (Westport, Conn., 1973) is excellent on the radical and socialist influences on Gompers' early development. Joseph R. Conlin, *Big Bill Haywood and the Radical Union Movement* (Syracuse, 1969) offers new insights about its subject. And Nick Salvatore, *Eugene V. Debs, Citizen and Socialist* (Urbana, 1982) is in a class by itself as a biography of a labor radical, one which integrates personal psycho-sexual analysis with sophisticated social and political history.

The history of strikes has also commanded a great deal of attention from historians, journalists, and even novelists. No better scholarly synthesis of the subject exists than P. K. Edwards, *Strikes in the United States, 1881–1974* (Oxford, 1981). For a more exciting and romantic version of the same story, one which lauds the revolutionary potential of spontaneous rank-and-file strikes, see Jeremy Brecher, *Strike!* (San Francisco, 1972). A more dyspeptic account can be found in Rhodri Jeffreys-Jones, *Violence and Reform in American History* (New York, 1978). Other fine studies of single industrial conflicts include the following: Wayne G. Broehl, Jr., *The Molly Maguires* (Cambridge, Mass., 1964); Robert V. Bruce, *1877: Year of Violence* (Indianapolis, 1959); Donald L. McMurray, *The Great Burlington Strike of 1888* (Cambridge, Mass., 1956); Henry David, *History of the Haymarket Affair* (New York, 1936); Almont Lindsay, *The Pullman Strike* (Chicago, 1942); and Leon Wolff, *Lockout: the Story of the Homestead Strike of 1892* (New York, 1965). For the great upheaval of 1919, one might best consult: David Brody, *Labor in Crisis: The Steel Strike of 1919* (Philadelphia, 1965); Francis Russell, *A City in Terror: 1919, The Boston Police Strike* (New York, 1975); and Robert L. Friedman, *The Seattle General Strike* (Seattle, 1964).

Beginning with the decade of the 1960s a generation of younger scholars sought to break out of the institutional mold of labor history. The first important study which placed American workers within the larger context of community structure and values was David Brody's *Steelworkers in America: The Nonunion Era* (Cambridge, Mass., 1960), a groundbreaking effort to locate steelworkers within the ethnic, occupational, and cultural parameters of the industry and the communities in which they labored and lived. Among the scholars who have followed the path blazed by Brody have been Irwin Yellowitz, whose *Labor and the Progressive Movement in New York State, 1897–1916* (Ithaca, 1965) coolly analyzes the coalition of convenience arranged between social reformers and trade unionists in New York and why it proved shaky; Graham Adams, Jr., whose *Age of Industrial Violence, 1910–1915: The Activities and Findings of the United States Commission on Industrial Relations* (New York, 1966) surveys with more detail than perception the social dynamite so carelessly strewn about Progressive America; Katherine Harvey's *The Best-Dressed Miners: Life and Labor in the Maryland Coal Region, 1835–1910*

(Ithaca, 1969) whose subtitle adequately describes the book's contents; Melvyn Dubofsky's *When Workers Organize: New York City in the Progressive Era* (Amherst, Mass., 1968), which attempts to set wage workers firmly within an urban community and to probe their relationship with other members of the community during a series of major industrial confrontations; and Alexander Saxton's *The Indispensable Enemy: Labor and the Anti-Chinese Movement in California* (Berkeley, 1971), an illuminating analysis of racialism's catastrophic effect on California workers and its ideological roots in Jacksonian thought and politics. Perhaps the most impressive of these more recent efforts to locate American workers within the larger community has been David Montgomery's *Beyond Equality: Labor and the Radical Republicans, 1862-1872* (New York, 1967), a many-faceted, subtle, and brilliantly orchestrated collection of hypotheses which actually raises more questions than it answers.

These scholars and those who subsequently followed the same paths had been enormously influenced by the work of European historians, especially a group of English scholars who stressed the influence of culture, tradition, and noneconomic factors on working-class behavior. The debt American labor historians owe to Edward P. Thompson for his *The Making of the English Working Class* (London, 1963) and his essay, "Time, Work-Discipline, and Industrial Capitalism," *Past and Present* 38 (1967), 56-97; and Eric J. Hobsbawm for his collection of essays, *Labouring Men* (London, 1964) can scarcely be repaid. But for attempts by Americans to apply the insights and approaches pioneered by Thompson and Hobsbawm, among other European historians, one should pay close attention to the following: Herbert G. Gutman, *Work, Culture, and Society in Industrializing America* (New York, 1976); David Montgomery, *Workers' Control in America* (New York, 1979); and the opening chapters of James R. Green, *The World of the Worker* (New York, 1980). In the same class but more traditional in some senses is David Brody's opening essay in *Workers in Industrial America* (New York, 1980). A collection of essays edited by Milton Cantor presents the contributions of some younger historians: *American Workingclass Culture: Explorations in American Labor and Social History* (Westport, Conn., 1979) as does another collection edited by Michael H. Frisch and Daniel J. Walkowitz, *Working-Class America: Essays on Labor, Community, and American Society* (Urbana, 1983).

The new approaches to labor history have been most assiduously applied to the study of social and occupational mobility, ethnicity, gender and race, and community history. So interrelated are the above themes that it is difficult to assign books to any particular category. Many historians followed the lead of Stephan Thernstrom who in *Poverty and Progress: Social Mobility in a Nineteenth Century City* (Cambridge, Mass., 1964) and *The Other Bostonians: Poverty and Progress in the American Metropolis* (Cambridge, Mass., 1973) focused on occupational and social mobility among working-class Americans. The best of the subsequent studies in that genre include Clyde and Sally Griffen, *Natives and Newcomers: The Ordering of Opportunity in Mid-Nineteenth Century Poughkeepsie* (Cambridge, Mass., 1978); Thomas Kessner, *The Golden Door: Italian and Jewish Immigrant Mobility in New York City, 1880–1915* (New York, 1977); Josef J. Barton, *Peasants and Strangers: Italians, Rumanians, and Slovaks in an American City* (Cambridge, Mass., 1975); and John Bodnar, et al., *Lives of their Own: Blacks, Italians, and Poles in Pittsburgh, 1900–1960* (Pittsburgh, 1982).

The literature on working-class ethnics continues to grow. Among older studies the following should not be missed: Rowland Berthoff, *British Immigrants in Industrial America, 1790–1950* (Cambridge, Mass., 1953); Clifton K. Yearly, *Britons in American Labor: A History of the Influence of the United Kingdom Immigrants on American Labor, 1820–1914* (Baltimore, 1957); Moses Rischin, *The Promised City: New York's Jews, 1870–1914* (Cambridge, Mass., 1962); and Humbert Nelli, *The Italians in Chicago, 1890–1930: A Study in Ethnic Mobility* (New York, 1970); Gerd Korman, *Industrialization, Immigrants, and Americanizers: The View from Milwaukee* (Madison, 1967). The best of the more recent ones include John Bodnar,

Immigration and Industrialization: Ethnicity in an American Mill Town, 1870-1940 (Pittsburgh, 1977); Tamara Hareven, *Family Time and Industrial Time: The Relationship between Family and Work in a New England Industrial Community* (New York, 1982); John Briggs, *An American Passage: Immigrants to Three American Cities* (New Haven, 1978); Dino Cinel, *From Italy to San Francisco: The Immigrant Experience* (Stanford, 1982); and Caroline Golab, *Immigrant Destinations* (Philadelphia, 1977), a study of Polish immigrants in the city of Brotherly Love.

Those particularly interested in the ethnic politics of the working class may find some revealing, if highly tendentious, discussions of late nineteenth-century working-class political behavior in Paul Klepner, *The Cross of Culture: A Social Analysis of Midwestern Politics, 1850-1900* (New York, 1970), and Richard Jensen, *The Winning of the Midwest: Social and Political Conflict, 1888-1896* (Chicago, 1971). Also see Samuel McSeveney, *The Politics of Depression: Political Behavior in the Northeast, 1893-1896* (New York, 1972).

The best of the community labor studies number Allan Dawley, *Class and Community: The Industrial Revolution in Lynn* (Cambridge, Mass., 1976); Daniel Walkowitz, *Worker City, Company Town: Iron and Cotton Worker Protest in Troy and Cohoes, New York, 1855-1884* (Urbana, 1978); John Cumbler, *Working-Class Community in Industrial America: Work, Leisure, and Struggle in Two Industrial Cities, 1880-1930* (Westport, Conn., 1979); David A. Corbin, *Life, Work, and Rebellion in the Coal Fields: The Southern West Virginia Coal Miners, 1880-1922* (Urbana, 1981); Roy A. Rosenzweig, *Eight Hours for What We Will: Workers and Leisure in an Industrial City, 1870-1920* (New York, 1983); and Olivier Zunz, *The Changing Face of Inequality: Urbanization, Industrial Development, and Immigrants in Detroit, 1880-1920* (Chicago, 1982). For two books that employ a similar approach but examine communities of workers rather than geographical places see Walter Licht, *Working for the Railroad: The Organization of Work in the Nineteenth Century* (Princeton, 1983) and James

Ducker, *Men of Steel Rails: Workers on the Atchison, Topeka, and Santa Fe Railroad, 1869-1900* (Lincoln, Neb., 1983). Finally, Leon Fink, *Workingmen's Democracy: The Knights of Labor and American Politics* (Urbana, 1983), combines community history with a new interpretation of the Knights of Labor. An excellent book which uses community history comparatively to examine real wages and standards of living in the U.S. and England is Peter Shergold, *Working-Class Life: The "American Standard" in Comparative Perspective, 1899-1913* (Pittsburgh, 1982).

No subject has engendered more interest and produced as much good literature recently as women's history. The best general historical treatment of women and work is now Alice Kessler-Harris, *Out to Work: A History of Wage-Earning Women in the United States* (New York, 1982). Equally complete but less easy to read are Philip Foner's two volumes, *Women and the American Labor Movement* (New York, 1979-1980), which have been synthesized in one volume of the same title (New York, 1982). Barbara Wertheimer's *We Were There: The Story of Working Women in America* (New York, 1977) is a popularly written version of the subject. An excellent collection of original documents can be found in Rosalyn Baxendall, et al., *America's Working Women: A Documentary History* (New York, 1976). Meredith Tax, *The Rising of the Women* (New York, 1980), examines the more radical aspects of women's labor history. More specialized studies number Leslie W. Tentler, *Wage-Earning Women: Industrial Work and Family Life in the United States, 1900-1930* (New York, 1979); Nancy Schrom Dye, *As Equals and as Sisters: Feminism, Unionism, and the Women's Trade Union League of New York* (Columbia, Mo., 1980); Maurine W. Greenwald, *Women, War, and Work: The Impact of World War I on Women Workers in the United States* (Westport, Conn., 1980); and two general histories of domestic service: David Katzman, *Seven Days a Week: Women and Domestic Service in Industrializing America* (New York, 1978); and Daniel E. Sutherland, *Americans and their Servants: Domestic Service in the United States from 1800 to 1920* (Baton

Rouge, 1981). Two recent books examine stereotypical women's occupations: Barbara Melosh, *"The Physician's Hand:" Work Culture and Conflict in American Nursing* (Philadelphia, 1982) and Margery Davies, *Woman's Place is at the Typewriter: Office Work and Office Workers, 1870-1930* (Philadelphia, 1982).

Several books provide solid introductions to the history of black workers. The most general, comprehensive, and easy to read is William H. Harris, *The Harder We Run: Black Workers since the Civil War* (New York, 1982). An old but valuable classic remains Sterling D. Spero and Abram L. Harris, *The Black Worker* (New York, 1931). Julius Jacobson, ed., *The Negro and the American Labor Movement* (New York, 1965) provides a set of essays largely critical of the racial policies of the trade unions. And, finally, Philip S. Foner, *Organized Labor and the Black Worker, 1619-1973* (New York, 1974) offers his customary encyclopedic, Marxist treatment of the subject.

One of the most fruitful topics for investigation has become the whole subject of corporate labor policies, including scientific management, technological change, company unionism, and welfare capitalism. Two books by economists who characterize themselves as Marxists provide the most controversial analyses of corporate labor policies and should not be ignored: Richard Edwards, *Contested Terrain: The Transformation of the Workplace in the Twentieth Century* (New York, 1979) and David Gordon, et al., *Segmented Work, Divided Workers* (New York, 1982). Two books by Daniel Nelson are especially good on managerial labor strategies: *Managers and Workers: The Origins of the New Factory System in the United States, 1880-1920* (Madison, Wis., 1975) and *Frederick W. Taylor and Scientific Management* (Madison, Wis., 1980). James Weinstein in *The Corporate Ideal in the Liberal State* (Boston, 1968) and Stuart Brandes, *American Welfare Capitalism, 1880-1940* (Chicago, 1976) treat just what their topics suggest. Stephen Meyer III examines the most famous and criticized of all the new managerial strategies, "Fordism," in *The Five-Dollar Day: Labor Management and Social Control in the Ford Motor Company, 1908-1921* (Albany, N.Y., 1981). Two equally interesting studies on aspects of the subject are Bruno Ramirez, *When Workers Fight: The Politics of Industrial Relations in the Progressive Era, 1898–1916* (Westport, Conn., 1978) and Irwin Yellowitz, *Industrialization and the American Labor Movement, 1850–1900* (Port Washington, N.Y., 1977). Two books that must not be neglected provide perceptive intellectual histories of the changing nature of work and the work ethic in the industrial era: Daniel T. Rodgers, *The Work Ethic in Industrial America, 1850–1920* (Chicago, 1978); and James B. Gilbert, *Work Without Salvation: America's Intellectuals and Industrial Alienation, 1880–1910* (Baltimore, 1977).

Yet as both David Brody, "The Old Labor History and the New: In Search of an American Working Class," *Labor History,* XX (Winter, 1979), 511–526, and David Montgomery, "To Study the People: The American Working Class," *Labor History,* XXI (Fall 1980), 485–512, emphasize, we still lack a synthesis of American labor history to replace the one originated by Commons and Perlman, which has fallen into disfavor among many historians. Perhaps as Robert Ozanne, one of the more committed and skilled practitioners of the older institutional approach has argued, we should all do our best to enrich the field of labor history. As he implies in "Trends in American Labor History," *Labor History,* XXI (Fall 1981), 513–521, it is time to declare a truce in the war between the "old" labor history and the "new" and get on with serious research.

INDEX